Fuller, Benjamin F., 1922-
American health care :
rebirth or suicide?
RA395.A3 F85 1994
c.2

DISCARDED

Y0-AIC-248

To Renew Books
PHONE: (925) 969-3100

ROBERT M. FISHER LIBRARY
JOHN F. KENNEDY UNIVERSITY
100 ELLINWOOD WAY
PLEASANT HILL, CA 94523

AMERICAN HEALTH CARE
Rebirth or Suicide?

ABOUT THE AUTHOR

Benjamin F. Fuller, M.D. is an internist. He served a fellowship at the Mayo Clinic from 1947–1950. He practiced in the community from 1951–1966 when he left private practice to join the faculty of the medical school on a full time basis (University of Minnesota). He was a founder of the Department of Family Practice in the medical school (which was the first such department in the United States) and was its first professor and head. He was also a professor in the Department of Internal Medicine and was a founder and the first head of the section of primary care in that department. He left the full time faculty in 1978 to resume community practice. He continued to teach on a part time basis. He was chief of staff at one of our large hospitals. He was a founder of one of our preferred provider organizations and was instrumental in the development of an HMO years before they were called HMOs.

AMERICAN HEALTH CARE

Rebirth or Suicide?

By

BENJAMIN F. FULLER, M.D.

CHARLES C THOMAS • PUBLISHER
Springfield • Illinois • U.S.A.

Published and Distributed Throughout the World by

CHARLES C THOMAS • PUBLISHER
2600 South First Street
Springfield, Illinois 62794-9265

This book is protected by copyright. No part of
it may be reproduced in any manner without
written permission from the publisher.

© *1994 by* CHARLES C THOMAS • PUBLISHER
ISBN 0-398-05914-4
Library of Congress Catalog Card Number: 94-9868

With THOMAS BOOKS *careful attention is given to all details of manufacturing and design. It is the Publisher's desire to present books that are satisfactory as to their physical qualities and artistic possibilities and appropriate for their particular use.* THOMAS BOOKS *will be true to those laws of quality that assure a good name and good will.*

Printed in the United States of America
SC-R-3

Library of Congress Cataloging-in-Publication Data

Fuller, Benjamin F., 1922–
American health care : rebirth or suicide? / by Benjamin F. Fuller.
p.   cm.
Includes bibliographical references.
ISBN 0-398-05914-4
1. Medical policy—United States.   2. Health care reform—United States.   3. Primary care (Medicine)—United States.   I. Title.
RA395.A3F85   1994
362.1'0973—dc20   94-9868
                                                                                                    CIP

PREFACE

Patient care in the United States is in an extremely critical position. This is hardly news to anyone who reads newspapers, magazines, or medical journals or who listens to or looks at the broadcast media. It is hardly news to anyone paying for health insurance during recent years.

What is news is the severity of the crisis and the nature of it. We all know that health care costs too much. We all know that more and more people are finding access to care increasingly limited. We all know that the competitiveness of American industry in pricing products is severely impaired by the amount of money it must spend on health care for its employees.

What seems to be less well known to the public and even to the medical profession is the depth of the crisis and its long-term ramifications if it is not resolved. In addition, I see little evidence that we even know what the true problem is, what caused it, and what to do about it.

That is the subject of this book.

Frank Fuller is a major contributor to this book. I wrote the initial script and take responsibility for all the positions taken in it. However, he edited and re-edited it to get it in its present form. I daresay, we passed the manuscript back and forth twenty or thirty times before he was satisfied with it. It is an interesting experience to have your son as a chief critic of your work. So, while I take full responsibility for the content, I want to give him full credit for the final form it took.

The other credits I would give are too numerous to mention. My contact with many of my teachers and colleagues over the years helped me develop my thoughts. Many of my friends and patients have discussed their views of events as they occurred, and these conversations gave me important insights. My wife, who has always been my mentor, was also a valuable contributor.

B. F. Fuller, M.D.

INTRODUCTION

Health care reform seems inevitable, and properly so. It is long overdue. Several major proposals have been forwarded. All of them have much that will improve the system. Most of the changes proposed in the plans deal with improving access and reducing cost, certainly vital factors.

All of the plans speak of increasing numbers of primary physicians. Primary physician has become the "buzz word" for patient care in the nineties. And, there is no doubt that the primary physician is critical to the success of health care reform. But simply increasing numbers is not enough for success. In fact, if increasing numbers is all that is done, I believe that failure is assured.

Two other things are necessary. The position of the primary physician in the medical hierarchy must be changed, both in the community and in the academic sector. It must be recognized and accepted that primary physicians are the managers of the total care of their patients with authority to control the use of technology when they think it is inappropriate for a particular patient.

For this to happen successfully, educational programs for primary physicians will have to be reformed. Some observers call the necessary educational changes "revolutionary." The reasons for the changes and the types of changes will be discussed in this book.

To understand these needs, one must consider the astounding development of specialization in every field, not just health care, over the past several decades. Specialization has increased the possibilities and effectiveness in every line of work. Unfortunately, it also has brought new kinds of problems. These problems are the result of the narrow, often short-term focus of specialists.

Peter Drucker, the well known authority on management, recognizes the great value of specialization and encourages it. But he warns of the dangers of this narrowing in diverting their vision from the "goals of the business." Drucker illustrates by means of the concept of "suboptimization."

As a guideline, he says the "optimization" of process and performance of one specialty or area must not be made at the expense of other specialties or areas. This constitutes undesirable suboptimization of the whole.

According to his theory of management, the remedy is found in the way decisions are made. Drucker believes that decisions should always be made at levels which insure that all activities and objectives affected are fully considered. In health care this means that many decisions that often are made at the specialty level should be made at the general level—or at the very least through active consultation with generalists. This is especially important when decisions will have a long lasting or broad impact, particularly when they deal with dilemmas.

One might ask how are generalists to play a larger role in medical decision making. It is through the use of the "team design" in management. Referring again to Drucker in his statements about the organization of teams of knowledge workers:

> Specialized knowledge is a fragment, if not mere "data". It becomes productive only if put together with other people's knowledge. It becomes effective only as input to other people's decisions, other people's work, other people's understanding. It becomes "results" only as a team.[1]

Thus in health care, when specialists are utilized, primary physicians must manage the total continuum of care. They must continue to be very active and often be the leading members of the teams of providers. It is the generalists who see the earliest manifestations of each patient's problem, who have a broad view of all organ systems, and who are familiar with all of the patient's problems. It is also the generalists who will continue to see their patients after specialty services are completed.

Medical education has expanded immensely in terms of its factual content, but it has failed to deal with the problems of comprehensive decision making in the milieu of increasing numbers and types of specialists. It is time that the academic leaders accept this responsibility.

---

[1]Peter D. Drucker, *Management: Tasks, Responsibilities, Practices,* Harper and Row, New York, 1974, 543, 567–571.

CONTENTS

	Page
Preface	v
Introduction	vii

CHAPTER ONE—HOW THE PROBLEMS DEVELOPED.   3
A history of the technologic advances of the past fifty years. How technologic advances affected patient care. A review of the socio-economic changes in patient care: increasing costs, reduced access, and possible rationing of resources—all unnecessary.

CHAPTER TWO—A PROFESSION COMMITTING SUICIDE.   15
The increasing power of specialists. The loss of status and diminishing role of primary physicians. The reasons for it. The reasons for general practice becoming virtually extinct. A definition of the three types of primary physicians. How they developed. The failure to teach primary physicians what they need to know to handle their new responsibilities.

CHAPTER THREE—BAD MEDICINE.   21
Failure to "diagnose the disease" destroying the socio-economic base of patient care. A definition of what that diagnosis is. What must be done to correct it.

CHAPTER FOUR—IF THE ONLY TOOL YOU HAVE IS A HAMMER, EVERYTHING LOOKS LIKE A NAIL.   31
How the subordination of the cognitive physicians (primary physicians) to the technologically trained physicians has led to the present inappropriate overutilization of resources.

CHAPTER FIVE—THE FOURTH REVOLUTION.   37
A description of the four revolutions in medical practice that have occurred in the United States this century and their implications. Special emphasis is placed on the revolution that is occurring now and what it could mean to the future of patient care. Who should control medical decision making?

CHAPTER SIX—THE ART OF MEDICINE.   43
The mystique surrounding the "art" of medicine and why that mystique is harmful. A definition of what the "art" really is. The socialization of medical students into the profession.

The difficulties medical students have accepting illness, death, and the limitations of medical knowledge. A comparison of entering and graduating medical students of the forties and fifties with today's students.

CHAPTER SEVEN — NEEDED: LOGICAL PROBLEM SOLVING SKILLS. ... 51

Patient care is an exercise in logical decision making. What cognitive skills must be taught for primary physicians to be effective practitioners. Medical and moral dilemmas: How they differ from each other and why the distinction is important.

CHAPTER EIGHT — TOO MANY COOKS.... 55

Who is in charge of critically ill patients? Why sometimes no one knows who is in charge. Who should be in charge? Some examples of what happens in the absence of proper definition.

CHAPTER NINE — HOPING SOMETHING WORKS. 63

The irrationality of treatment based only on the hope that it will work. How to avoid that trap. How fear of error influences decision making. The dangers of indiscriminate screening, and how this can be avoided.

CHAPTER TEN — EVERYTHING HAS BEEN DONE THAT CAN BE DONE. 73

Why this old cliche is not only inapplicable today but is regressive. Pressures on physicians to act. The importance of communication skills to physicians. Why more emphasis must be placed on teaching communication skills.

CHAPTER ELEVEN — THE DECLINE OF PROFESSIONALISM. 79

Why professional status is given, why physicians are losing it, and the implications of this loss.

CHAPTER TWELVE — WHAT'S NEXT? 83

Issues that must be faced if beneficial change is to occur.

CHAPTER THIRTEEN — FACING UP TO REALITY. 87

Medicine is a social science as well as a high tech science. Why revolutionary action will be necessary to achieve effective changes in educational programs for primary physicians. What the changes must include.

CHAPTER FOURTEEN — A CALL TO ACTION. 97

How the changes can be implemented.

CHAPTER FIFTEEN — CONCLUSION. 101

AMERICAN HEALTH CARE
Rebirth or Suicide?

Chapter One

HOW THE PROBLEMS DEVELOPED

I am writing this monograph to the public. Physicians may also find it interesting. I hope they will.

Health care in America has become one of the most widely discussed areas in government, and rightly so. It is far too expensive, and it is not available to a large segment of the population. Even those who have adequate coverage are always at risk of losing it.

This situation has been developing for many years. We look at it as something new, but it actually goes back at least to the early 1950s although it was not widely recognized as a problem at that time. I want to review how it has developed and then suggest some solutions that have not yet been proposed.

My father died of a heart attack in 1945. He was hospitalized in one of the leading hospitals in St. Paul in a large single room. After his death, I became the administrator of his estate and settled his hospital bill. The total cost of his hospital care was $8.50 per day. This included everything except the physician's fee. He had good care. Everything that could be done had been done. However, at that time, there was not much to do. He had a chest x-ray, electrocardiograms as necessary, and a few blood tests.

Compare that to the present time. The vast array of diagnostic tests and treatments can run the costs of hospitalization for a heart attack to thousands of dollars per day.

The point of this is that decisions in patient care are much more difficult today. The old cliche that "everything has been done that *can* be done" is no longer applicable and should not be invoked. Rather, the saying must be that "everything has been done that *should* be done." I believe that this is an important part of our problem. We could use everything that was available in 1945 and still be practicing good medicine because not much was available. We did not have to worry about rejecting some forms of testing or treatment. Today, with the massive technology available, we have to make decisions not to do some things.

These decisions are much more difficult and require special kinds of education in order to make them skillfully. If they are not made skillfully, quality of patient care will suffer. It does not matter whether the error is doing too much (error of commission) or doing too little (error of omission). Either way, the patient is at risk of being harmed.

This means that exemplary patient care in our high technology environment requires that an entirely new kind of physician be developed. These physicians must be prepared to be the manager of the total care of their patients, whether they are providing the care directly or whether they are using consultants to provide part of it. This is what the primary physician must do if costs are to be controlled while enhancing quality. The modern primary physician must be the key player, not just a "gatekeeper." This is what the battle has been about since 1966 when this concept was first defined in the Millis Report.[1]

I graduated from medical school in 1945, was an intern in 1946, and finished a fellowship in internal medicine at the Mayo Clinic in 1950. Since that time, I have engaged in community practice and have always been involved in medical education. My experience in medical education was on a part time basis most of my career and on a full time basis from 1966 to 1977. I saw the problems developing. Let's look at a brief history of the past forty-five years.

How much the practice of medicine has changed in just one professional lifetime! The magnitude of these changes is probably not fully appreciated by the public. Even many younger physicians may not appreciate the dynamism physicians my age have lived through. We practiced in what has been called the "Golden Age of Medicine," and it truly was a golden age in terms of scientific advances. It seemed that new discoveries were made every day in all fields of medicine. Entirely new fields were opened (immunochemistry, organ transplants, cardiopulmonary resuscitation, to name only a few).

Unfortunately, the enthusiasm generated by the new discoveries was never matched by any enthusiasm to learn how to use them most effectively. Because of that, we face the very real possibility of diminished benefits from many of those advances in the next professional lifetime.

A simple review of some of these changes will show how much could be lost if the current problems are not resolved.

---

[1] Report of the Citizen's Commission on Graduate Medical Education, Council on Medical Education, American Medical Assn., 1966.

THE FORTIES

This was a watershed decade. Medical practice was unbelievably different from today, and the approach to many problems seems primitive by today's standards.

For example, syphilis was treated with bismuth and arsenic and, in certain advanced forms, with malaria injections. These were toxic treatments and were only marginally effective. Those who contracted syphilis were correct to be frightened of both the disease and the treatment.

Lobar pneumonia was treated with pneumococcal serum, and, even when treated, had a high mortality rate. It was called "the old person's friend" because it provided a fairly quick and merciful death for many weakened by other diseases. Modern antibiotics have largely taken this friend away.

Pernicious anemia, now treated with Vitamin B_{12}, was treated with liver extract injections, a major advance over eating raw liver. There was no treatment for cancer except surgery, and this was effective in only a limited number of patients. Heart failure was treated with ground up foxglove (digitalis) leaf and with injections of mercury. While moderately effective, it did not compare to modern treatment. When oxygen was necessary, it was usually given in an oxygen tent, an inefficient and cumbersome method.

The "iron lung" was a major advance in the treatment of severely ill polio patients, but it was not a curative measure. The polio epidemics were terrifying.

Sulfa drugs were used in some infections and were very toxic (sometimes fatal) if used improperly. Penicillin was available in limited amounts to the armed forces and for research but not to the general public.

Ulcers were treated with milk and antacids, and the so called "white diets"—eggs, fish, pureed food, cream of wheat, etc.—were popular as well. Severe ulcer disease was frequently treated with extensive stomach surgery.

Cataracts were treated surgically with hospitalizations lasting up to six weeks. During much of that time, patients were kept immobile. Death and complications were frequent. Today, most patients go home the same day as the surgery.

Patients with heart attacks were hospitalized for up to eight weeks. Now, the hospitalization is usually less than two weeks.

Severe (life threatening) hypertension was treated with a radical nerve cutting operation that had a high mortality, substantial post operative morbidity, and limited benefits. Statistically, one-third of patients died of the operation, one third were helped, and one third were unchanged. There were no effective drugs for hypertension.

Tuberculosis was treated with a minimum of nine months in a sanatorium. There was also extensive surgical treatment for tuberculosis which was of very limited value. No effective drugs were available.

Disease caused by an overactive thyroid gland could only be treated surgically, and the operation was very dangerous.

And this list could go on and on. But the end of World War II was the beginning of almost miraculous changes. Several antibiotics became available by 1950, and intensive research was being done to develop effective drugs to treat high blood pressure and cancer. Anticoagulants were developed for treating blood clotting disorders, and the ravages of syphilis and rheumatic fever were suppressed by penicillin. Treatment of heart failure was becoming more effective and rational.

That was the environment in which physicians my age learned medicine, and, despite the many limits of medicine, there was much satisfaction during the 1940s. Physicians had many successes, and the relationship between the physicians and their patients was very good. The medical profession and individual physicians were held in high esteem by the public. Their professional ranking was at the top of the various polls that were conducted at the time, a sharp contrast to the situation today.

THE FIFTIES

Diagnostic and treatment potential had improved considerably. Multiple antibiotics were developed, making the treatment of infections much more effective. The treatment of heart attacks was improving, and drugs to retard blood clotting were being used very successfully. Hospital stays for heart attacks were shortened to three weeks, and patients were allowed to become active sooner. Advances were being made in the diagnosis of heart disease as well as in x-ray diagnosis. Surgical techniques were becoming more sophisticated as well.

Open heart surgery was being pioneered to great acclaim. At that time, the heart was the symbol of life. When it stopped, life ended. So surgery on the heart had a great symbolic and shock value. The frontiers of medicine seemed limitless.

Polio vaccines were developed and made widely available. Those old enough to remember the polio epidemics remember what relief the vaccines brought. Another disease conquered.

Public health programs pushed for mass vaccination to control many diseases.

Along with these amazing discoveries, the socioeconomic forces squeezing the health care system were becoming visible. Health insurance covering surgical and diagnostic procedures performed in hospitals was a growing industry. However, it paid little or nothing for routine office visits or for tests not done in the hospital. This led to more frequent hospitalizations and indiscriminate and unnecessary testing and really was the beginning of the cost spiral we see today. I believed then, and still do, that on any given day I could have reviewed the charts of patients in hospitals and discharged at least half of them without causing them harm. Patients were frequently hospitalized for such vague symptoms as fatigue, neck pain, or back pain.

This was when the specter of inappropriate utilization of medical resources was becoming apparent to many inside the profession. Costs were rising and patients and insurers were complaining. This had not yet affected business or government, but it was beginning to have a severe impact on those with too much income to qualify for charity but not enough to be able to afford the cost of illness. Most of these people were uninsured or had very low paying insurance policies. Many of the aged fell into this group.

In 1952, the cost of a bed in a double room in one of our leading hospitals was $16. This did not include any other services and it increased to $18.50 by 1954. This doesn't seem like much today, but it was a lot then. People were complaining bitterly about cost. Group Health (Minnesota), a staff model pre-paid plan (what is now called an HMO) was created in response to these kinds of costs.

It was a turbulent decade, and this turbulence existed in most areas of the country. It was the beginning of a continuing struggle by cognitive physicians—physicians who were skilled diagnosticians and decision makers—primarily internists and pediatricians at that time—to gain more recognition for their efforts. This struggle was for greater professional recognition, but it took the form of an effort for greater pay equity with the technologic physicians. I was involved in this struggle. Insurance companies were our adversaries because they paid more for hospitalizations and technological interventions than they did for office visits, physical examinations and non-technological treatment. It was a bitter struggle and resulted in some bruises. I have always believed that this struggle resulted in Blue Shield of Minnesota going out of business as an independent company and ending up as part of Blue Cross.

Although the public cannot be expected to be sympathetic to physicians' complaints about pay, the ultimate result of these policies was to diminish the status, effectiveness, and numbers of today's primary physicians and general diagnosticians.

Adding to the complexity of the period, general practice was dying. Fewer and fewer students were selecting it as a career. This led general practitioners then in practice to organize and develop a powerful political lobby to try to reverse the trend.

In response to some of these problems, quality assurance programs were beginning to be developed in hospitals. They usually consisted of a chart review by individual physicians who followed a series of questions to be answered. They were very simplistic, but it was a beginning.

These years, the late forties and fifties, heralded the golden age of medicine.

THE SIXTIES

The sixties were an extension of the fifties with further advances in medical technology and even sharper cost increases. The problems were becoming apparent to everyone by now.

Transplant surgery was moving out of the experimental, pioneering stages. Cardiac surgeons like Lillehei, Barnard, and DeBakey were becoming international heroes. Birth control pills were being used widely. New treatments for cancer were being tested.

In 1966 Medicare and Medicaid became law. This was a tremendous aid to the elderly and the poor. Although they never covered all the costs of care, they covered a higher proportion then than now. They also provided the elderly and poor with more dignity because they were now empowered to select a physician and hospital of their own choice instead of being arbitrarily assigned to one.

These programs affected medical schools because their main source of patients had been the city and county hospitals. These were mostly the elderly and the poor. Now these people had other options, leaving medical schools with fewer patients.

In my opinion, the end of the 1960s marked the beginning of the end of the golden age of medicine. During this decade, medical schools were becoming extremely specialty oriented, to the point where it was becoming an obvious problem. An increasing number of medical students in each succeeding class were selecting narrow specialty work rather than primary care specialties. There were many reasons for this, but one of the main reasons was that the students lacked role models of physicians with broad clinical skills while in medical school and in their residency training. Their main exposure was to highly technological subspecialists and researchers. Another reason was failure of medical educators to recognize the need for the re-defined primary physician of the Millis Report and establish suitable educational programs. In my opinion, these are the reasons for the dearth of primary physicians today.

Although the advances in medical research led to the scientific and technical advances of the decade, the dark side of this was that students were learning to intervene without learning how to evaluate the need for intervention. The technology was there, so use it. Lost in the shuffle was the question of appropriate use. This is the deficiency in the education of medical students and residents, and the lack of this kind of education is a major force in driving all costs upwards.

When I joined the medical school faculty full time in 1966, all of these things were just happening. Despite the clamor from outside, the medical school faculty members, with only a few exceptions, were adamantly opposed to reversing the trend toward training increasingly narrow subspecialists.

THE SEVENTIES

Although there continued to be many technological advances in medicine, the seventies marked the time when the social and economic side of the health care industry gained more attention. Costs were obviously out of control.

The last half of the sixties and the early seventies were when family practice programs were being organized nationwide. This was a bitter time in medicine, because the movement pitted the highly organized Academy of General Practice against the medical schools. There was bitter strife within the medical schools between those who favored the status quo and those who wanted to de-emphasize the training of subspecialists. The Academy of General Practice fought those who thought general practitioners were becoming anachronisms in an increasingly technologic age and should be replaced with better trained primary physicians. As the organizer and head of the newly formed Department of Family Practice and Community Health at Minnesota, I found myself in the middle, disagreeing with many of my colleagues on the faculty for wanting to go too far in one direction and with the Academy of General Practice for wanting to go too far in another direction. In Minnesota the struggle became extremely political.

The central issue was whether the new family practitioner should simply be a general practitioner better trained in the new technologies or whether an entirely new body of knowledge should be developed for this new specialty. Historically, general practice graduate students rotated from one service to another, spending several months in the departments of medicine, surgery, pediatrics, obstetrics, etc. I was advocating that the new Department of Family practice at Minnesota develop its own new and self-contained curriculum and teaching staff so that the students would not simply know a little about a lot of specialties. Instead, they would have concentrated teaching of disease medicine but also concentrated teaching of the development of clinical skills such as interviewing, decision making, medical sociology, and risk benefit analysis in a highly technological environment.

In other words, those of us who created the Family Practice Department wanted to develop a purely cognitive primary physician and eliminate all procedural training like surgery and obstetrics from the program. This physician would know when to use consultants and how to use them to obtain maximum benefit. They would truly be managers of the total care of their patients.

This led to a political battle which I lost, and the program at Minnesota still sends its residents from department to department with no strong central teaching of a body of knowledge unique to family practice.

The seventies were also the time when prepaid health plans (now called HMOs) surged in popularity. With the exception of the Kaiser plans which started during World War II on the west coast, the greatest growth of these plans has been in Minnesota. This is interesting to me, because in the late sixties and early seventies I tried to develop a prepaid plan to be used to attract a stable and representative patient population for the Department of Family Practice. At that time, prepayment was not popular within the medical profession, and the plan was successfully opposed by organized medicine at all levels. Four insurance companies were involved in helping develop it, and some aspects of the plan are still being used by these companies.

At the beginning of the seventies, about four percent of Minnesotans were insured by prepaid plans. Now the figure is about fifty percent.

These were the main actions of the seventies. In addition, costs were still rising.

THE EIGHTIES

In the eighties, it was becoming clear that many of the gains made during the past decades were becoming less available because we could not pay for them. The affluent and those with good health insurance might be able to afford them, but many, including many in the middle class, were finding it more difficult to obtain affordable health care.

The eighties became the decade of managed care. It also became the decade when most physicians lost some of their professional status by default. The profession's continuing inability to use technology rationally may ultimately lead to loss of all professional status for all physicians.

This was the decade when the benefits of the past should have become more easily available, but it didn't work out that way.

Why didn't it work out? The lack of success in controlling costs has been a primary cause. Almost in desperation, insurers, industry, and government have directed their cost control efforts at suppressing utilization of medical resources. Some of these efforts have merit, but many are arbitrary. Some of them are merely "nit picking" and serve only to infuriate physicians. Some are clearly obstructive with the apparent goal of delaying action to the point where the services will not be provided or delaying payment to the point where it becomes too much trouble to continue to seek reimbursement.

One common technique has serious implications. It is called "incentives" to not utilize and it is tied to reimbursement of physicians. Their income is dependent in part on their ability to reduce expenditures, and it goes under the euphemism of "risk sharing." In its extreme form, it can cause physicians to lose large sums of money simply on the "luck of the draw." That is, if one of their patients has a disease that requires use of expensive tools for diagnosis and treatment, a physician can lose a large amount of money because only a fixed amount of money is available for that patient's care. This enables the insurer to charge a smaller premium and be more competitive. Large insurers can factor these unusual expenses into their premiums so they don't lose money, but small groups of physicians are unable to do this.

The question that should be asked is, "How relevant are payment mechanisms (whether fee for service, managed care, prepayment, national health insurance) to the cost of care?" The answer, of course, is not at all. *Recent history demonstrates this, since all the devices used to control costs have failed so far.* Costs continue to rise!

The *critical* factor in cost and quality of medical care is the competence and integrity of the physicians making medical decisions. Regardless of the complexity of each patient's problem, there is a point at which further testing adds no more useful information. In fact, going beyond this point with further testing not only doesn't add useful information, it often confuses the issue. Of course, not reaching the point of optimal utilization is equally bad. Working with inadequate information also harms the patient. In other words, exceeding the point of optimal utilization is inappropriate overutilization while not reaching it is inappropriate underutilization. Both are potentially harmful.

Inappropriate overutilization reduces quality by increasing the frequency of iatrogenic (physician induced) problems due to the inherent risks of tests and treatment. In other words, patients are put at risk of complications without commensurate gain in benefit.

Inappropriate underutilization (withholding necessary tests or treatments) reduces quality by not providing the patient with what is needed. In this situation, patients are placed at risk of inadequate care without commensurate gain in benefit.

The financial incentives are to overutilize in the fee for service sector (the more you do, the more you get paid) and to underutilize in the prepaid (HMO) sector (the less you do, the more you get paid). There is no question about this.

My point is that, *regardless of payment mechanism,* proper decisions regarding utilization are dependent on the competence and integrity of the physician making the decisions. There is no magic formula that alters this fact.

So it is ironic that *the only approach not yet tried is to examine the medical school curriculum to see how well primary physicians are prepared to meet their new responsibilities in today's changing medical environment.*

What needs to be emphasized is that what physicians "sell" to patients is the ability to make good medical decisions. This takes priority over carrying out those decisions, although effective implementation is obviously important. This was a radical concept in the sixties when it was first being emphasized by a few teachers of family practice and internal medicine. It remains a radical concept today. Medical educators failed to recognize the importance of this, and, inevitably, the golden age of medicine began to fade.

Physicians do not sell surgery or pills or high tech wizardry or longevity. These are merely spin-offs from the data gathered by talking with patients and examining them, then evaluating them in the context of their total life situation. After that, the outcome is determined by picking the most suitable option based on risks and benefits.

Sometimes many things *can* be done, but often nothing *should* be done. Many physicians and some patients still can't make this transition. Not addressing this deficit in reasoning is a major failure of medical education.

Chapter Two

A PROFESSION COMMITTING SUICIDE

Many proposals have been made to try to contain costs. They have included increasing competition among providers of care, managed care, imposing external controls on utilization, and many other variations of these.

During the past year, we have seen the development of a plan for national health insurance which will be debated intensely over the coming years. Minnesota has developed a plan for local use. The American Association for Retired Persons has developed a plan for national health insurance which has much merit.

All of these plans have much in common. They all emphasize the importance of prevention. They all incorporate many of the features of current managed care programs to control utilization. They all call for increased numbers of primary physicians to act as "gatekeepers" for the plans.

What worries me is that these are attempts to provide simplistic solutions for very complex problems. We already know that the earlier solutions employed by managed care programs were inadequate as cost control measures. They had to be tried, and they helped a little, but costs have continued to rise at an unacceptable rate.

Recent emphasis on the importance of primary physicians is encouraging, but so far those who are advocating that we train more primary physicians (general internists, general pediatricians, and family practitioners) do not impress me that they really understand what the role of the primary physician should be in modern patient care. If they do not understand that, the training of more primary physicians will not make any difference. In fact, it could make matters worse.

Defining primary physicians' responsibilities and how they must be prepared educationally to assume those responsibilities is what this book is about. My arguments are based on the historic development of serious problems which could have been easily averted any time during the past thirty or forty years.

The medical profession's behavior toward its constituency during the past forty years has been that of a group with a death wish. It began in subtle ways shortly after World War II, but for at least the past twenty-five years has become more and more obvious to most of the public and to many within the profession. It is apparent in many ways. Physicians as a group frequently act with arrogance and insensitivity to the needs of patients. Despite clear signals that the public was becoming ever more disenchanted with the impersonal and technologically focused diagnosis and treatment they received as patients, organized medicine and the medical education establishment refused to acknowledge any deficits.

It was clear to some physicians and to a few perceptive non-physicians that the profession was in deep trouble by the late 1950s and early 1960s. Many papers and several seminal reports were published during those years. Except for passing lip service, all were ignored.

This continues to be true to the present time. Organized medicine and most medical educators have effectively "stonewalled" all efforts to effect substantive reform in the hierarchical structure of medical practice and of academic medicine. This has resulted in the chaos we see today. I am afraid that the problems will soon be irreversible unless revolutionary changes occur in both arenas.

And they must occur simultaneously if they are to be effective in preventing the death of the medical profession and patient care as we knew it (I am deliberately speaking in the past tense). I am not speaking of protecting any particular payment mechanism or other economic factors. I am speaking of preserving and even enhancing quality beyond what we have had in the past. This is independent of payment mechanisms and is totally dependent on proper education (which is deficient today). It is also dependent on change in the attitudes of organized medicine and community practitioners toward the cognitive aspects of patient care.

So far, most of the action has come from third party payers (insurers, including government). Because of the prohibitive cost escalation, they have directed their efforts toward reducing unit cost of services and reducing numbers of units provided. The methods used in doing this will be discussed later in this book. The arbitrary nature of some of the strictures placed on physician decision making has raised questions of maintenance of quality that are as yet unanswered. However, something had to be done, and these cost reduction efforts have had some successes.

My argument with the payers is not that unit costs are unimportant, but that they do not also examine aggregate cost of illness for a given individual over time. I have seen many cost accountings of individual services per visit (unit costs) provided by each physician. I have seen very few accountings of total cost for patients in a primary physician's practice calculated over a span of years (aggregate costs). And these attracted little attention. This is important, because more time spent assessing a patient's needs in the context of his or her total life situation enables physicians to be more judicious when they order procedures of all types. It also enables them to be more judicious in their prescribing habits. In other words, decreasing unit costs of some services to force physicians to see more patients per hour will inevitably diminish their capacity to make good decisions. This will result in greater utilization of diagnostic and therapeutic procedures, thereby increasing costs for unnecessary services. Sometimes it will result in services not being performed which should be, also increasing aggregate cost.

For example, consider a middle aged or older patient with chest pain that is not completely typical. The question here is whether it is caused by heart disease or not. The decisions to be made include whether or not to employ invasive (translate to risky and expensive) diagnostic procedures before deciding whether coronary artery bypass surgery is advisable (also risky and expensive).

Such evaluations are often very complex and time consuming. They involve making as accurate a diagnosis as possible, but also involve careful risk benefit analysis at each step of the way to decide if a particular test or treatment is in this individual patient's best interest. It is not an easy task. When insurers resist paying for the additional time spent in making such an evaluation, they are controlling unit costs. However, they are increasing aggregate costs at the same time. A careful evaluation requiring perhaps $150 worth of time may save thousands of dollars by avoiding unnecessary tests and procedures. Needless to say, quality of care is also enhanced.

When one looks at the estimate that thirty to thirty-five percent of procedures done are unnecessary, it becomes apparent that better education of primary physicians for their managerial responsibilities is mandatory if effective cost reduction is to occur. I want to emphasize that the cost of the procedures is only part of the total cost. The other cost, which never gets into the estimates, is the cost of correcting the damage done by complications of the procedures that were unnecessary. Nothing in medicine is risk free.

The diminution and ultimate extinction of the role of the primary physician as a decision maker and manager of patient care is the key to this crisis. For years, at an accelerating rate, the cognitive care and broad clinical skills provided by primary physicians have been made subordinate to the technical side of medicine. This is what will lead to the death of effective medical practice. There are many who will say that this is not happening and that primary care practitioners are in great demand. They will say that efforts are being made to increase the numbers of medical students to choose primary care as a career.

My response is that more must be done than is being done. At present, efforts to recruit primary physicians mostly take the form of various enticements such as partial forgiveness of tuition, partial forgiveness of student debt, and job placement. These are superficial rewards for commitment to a difficult lifetime career. Such enticements have failed for decades. I think they will continue to fail. Something different is needed.

Primary care is more widely discussed than it is understood. It is a relatively new designation of function of certain physicians. The Millis Report, published in 1966, coined and defined the term. This will be referred to later in this book in more detail. For now, I will only say that, although the term has become widely used, the definition of the Millis Report was never implemented. In a sense, the modern primary physician has become a paper tiger with lots of lip service and no real authority.

What are primary physicians? In current usage, they are generalists (general internists, family practitioners, or general pediatricians). This has not always been so. Not understanding the evolution of the generalist in medicine is a major factor in our present troubles. Let's look back to a different period.

We really don't have to look back too far, only to the 1930s or so.

Before the 1930s, the general practitioner was the dominant practitioner in the United States. General practice was a broad field including surgery, internal medicine, pediatrics, obstetrics, and, to a lesser extent, most of the other fields of patient care. The breadth of the field was really determined by the needs of the individual practitioner and the community in which he practiced (women physicians were uncommon then). Rural practitioners tended to be broader in function than urban practitioners because they were more isolated. In fact, general practice was almost unique to the United States. According to some medical historians, it developed because of the needs of the frontier and reached its fruition at a time when the frontier no longer existed. Once this happened, the historic general practitioner was no longer needed and specialty practice began to develop in earnest. General practice began to wither.

The two other primary care specialties were also quite broad. Internal medicine and pediatrics developed early and were broad cognitive specialties. In fact, some of the first internists embraced all age groups in their practices. Sir William Osler, a notable internist in the United States around the turn of the century, was an example of this in that he cared for both adults and children.

From the 1930s on, the three primary care specialties became better defined. This was a natural development but was enhanced by the development of certifying boards for internal medicine and pediatrics. Specialty designation in these two specialties required an extended period of training beyond medical school (an internship and three years of residency work under supervision). It also required passing an extensive examination. General practitioners continued to enter practice after one (or sometimes two) years of internship.

Initially, virtually all internists and pediatricians in community practice were generalists within their fields. A few developed special interests such as cardiology, gastroenterology, etc., and became known in the community as consultants in these areas, but most of their practices continued to be general internal medicine and pediatrics. While they acted as consultants in their field, they saw most patients directly without referral. The result of this is that the field of general practice began to erode and fewer medical students were selecting general practice as a career. This erosion was accelerated by World War II and the needs of the military. It continued for several decades.

The fields that came to be called primary care specialties carried heavy responsibilities through the decade of the 1950s, and their education was adequate to the challenge. These physicians spent sufficient time with their patients to accumulate data which enabled them to make accurate decisions. Then came the explosive development of medical technology followed by an equally explosive development of highly specialized, narrow subspecialties. The body of knowledge necessary to remain proficient in these new subspecialties became deeper and deeper but also narrower and narrower.

After that, the situation began to change. As the subspecialties continued their accelerated growth, and as medical technology developed new techniques and treatments in all fields, the challenge to the general internists, general pediatricians, and family practitioners (developed from general practice) became almost insurmountable. While their education in medical advances kept pace with the developments, education for their managerial responsibilities in a much more complex environment lagged. New fields of study to aid them in their decision making were not incorporated into their curriculum.

By the late 1960s, some physician educators were dividing physicians into two groups called conceptually oriented (or cognitive) physicians and technologically oriented (or procedural) physicians and were calling for a redefinition of generalism and additional education for it. Unfortunately, this has yet to happen. Until it happens, medical practice will suffer from the absence of a sufficient number of capable and objective managers of total, ongoing care of individual patients.

The result of this deficit is reduction of quality and increasing cost. More attention must be given by medical organizations and medical educators to the need for developing a cadre of physicians able to manage expertly the total care of individual patients in a complex and ever changing environment. Otherwise, much inappropriate utilization of resources will continue.

We have talked about preparation of the primary physician for the task. We have also talked about additional ways of counting the costs incurred by individual physicians.

What else must be done? Authority and responsibility of primary physicians must be redefined. Those who are prepared should be accepted as managers of the total care of their patients. Action on this must be taken by the medical community as a whole.

None of these suggestions are new. Most of them have been made repeatedly by many people over at least the past thirty years. The fact that they have been ignored for so long is a failure of all physicians and less so of the third party payers for medical care. That is the reason I spoke of the profession having a death wish in the initial paragraph. The "patient" is critical, and, unless we do something, will soon "go down the tube" to use the jargon of intensive care.

Chapter Three

BAD MEDICINE

Treating Symptoms Instead of the Disease: Prescription for Failure

Modern medicine is on a collision course with its myth and its reality. Most people are familiar with its miracles and its myths of miracle cures, but many of us are now becoming familiar with the reality that the system is slowly going bankrupt and that nothing is working to reverse that trend. Companies are paying higher costs for health insurance benefits (often affecting their competitive positions in international markets), employees are paying higher deductibles, patients are confronting rationing of resources, and those without good insurance coverage are experiencing less access. Large numbers of people have no health insurance at all.

In early 1991, two separate publications addressed this reality. *The Wall Street Journal* listed and discussed the failures of the various cost control methods that have been tried over the last fifteen to twenty years. In that article, one analyst admitted that every attempt to control health care costs has failed, and the article then went on to project that medical benefits would cost companies $22,000 per employee per year by the year 2000 if things remain the same.

At the same time, the American College of Physicians published in its newspaper, *The Observer,* that one in three of its members believes that the health care system works poorly and needs a major overhaul. Only two percent think the system works well. This is an ominous sign from a body of physicians who make up a major component of health care providers.

All in all, the reality is that the public's interests are not being served very well by the health care professions.

This is why health care reform has become a battle cry for the Clinton administration, some state governments (including Minnesota), and major national organizations (as AARP). These plans are carefully thought out. They all emphasize that we need more primary physicians. The major deficit that I see in the ones that I have examined is that they only deal with increasing numbers of primary physicians. They do not deal explicitly enough with the need for expanding their education to make them more effective.

The thesis of this book is that medical students and residents are not taught many things that they will need to know when they become practitioners. Instead, they are taught to rely heavily on medical technology, most of it expensive and some of it dangerous. This is because those who teach and do research lead an insular medical career that effectively prevents them from experiencing the realities of medical practice in a community. Yet, they control medical education. They teach students and decide what should be taught. They are virtually the only role models for medical students, and they are largely the determinants of each medical student's ultimate career choice.

For these reasons, academic physicians are a major cause of the crisis the health care system is facing today. A few examples demonstrate that statement. These examples are not unusual patients or problems. They are typical and well within the range of problems often seen in the community. They simply help explain how inadequately prepared physicians can be for handling their responsibilities.

For instance, a twenty-five year old woman developed typical symptoms of infectious hepatitis. So typical, in fact, that no one questioned the diagnosis during the first week of her illness. A week later, her course was reviewed by her physicians, and it was not quite as typical. Still, they continued to think it was hepatitis.

Over the next several days, however, her clinical course deviated even more from the usual, so the physicians in charge decided they would be more comfortable if they did a liver biopsy on her. This would confirm the diagnosis of hepatitis and was a proper decision at the time it was made. Unfortunately, this good decision was never implemented.

A gastroenterologist was called to do the biopsy. This is when the problems began. He was seeing the patient fairly late in the course of her illness and was looking at her problems from a limited perspective. He did not agree that it was hepatitis. He thought it was obstructive jaundice caused by a stone in the common bile duct or pancreatic cancer. He wanted to do another test where they place a needle into the bile duct and take x-rays instead of the biopsy. The radiologist he called was unable to enter the bile duct and therefore correctly concluded that the duct was not dilated and not obstructed.

This did not satisfy the gastroenterologist. He then decided to do something even more invasive, namely put a tube down her mouth, through the esophagus, stomach and duodenum, and into the common bile duct. This is such an invasive and risky procedure that a surgeon must be available when it is done in case of harm to the patient. So the test was done and showed no dilatation of the common bile duct. By this time, another week had gone by and the patient was clearly getting better. Her symptoms were again running the course of infectious hepatitis.

This situation was brought up in a seminar I chaired, and I became quite irritated. I told the primary physician in charge, a younger staff doctor, that he had to take a stronger position in situations like this because he had been seeing the patient over a period of time and knew more about her disease. I told him he should not have yielded to the opinion of the gastroenterologist who did not have that background.

I also argued that the first test done should have been a liver biopsy. That was why the gastroenterologist had been called. A liver biopsy is relatively safe and usually conclusive. Then, if there is still some question about her diagnosis, more complex tests can be done.

Some of the residents attending the seminar argued with me. They were afraid they might be missing an obstruction and were even awed somewhat by the gastroenterologist's actions and status.

I asked them what the obstruction could possibly be? Cancer of the pancreas in a twenty-five year old? Possible, but very, very rare in someone that young. A common duct stone? Possible, but unlikely in the absence of typical pain. In the absence of infection, it would be safe to wait and see. I was asking them to think this through.

The logical thing to do was to test for hepatitis first. The physician in charge reneged in his responsibility to the patient by following an illogical recommendation. He yielded too easily to the consultant and allowed the patient to endure two unnecessary and dangerous tests.

Another example of the public not being served well involves house calls. Patients rarely think of asking doctors to make house calls any more. This change occurred during the 1960s and was the result of public education that house calls were ineffective because they were so "low tech." This related to the growing reliance on diagnostic tests, many of which cannot be done in homes easily.

So now patients either put off calling their doctors until the week-end is over or go to emergency rooms where many tests are available if they are needed. It seems to matter little that the decision about going to the hospital for further testing could easily be made by a visit to the home most of the time. Sometimes this would result in a visit to the emergency room, but many times it would not. Since emergency room visits are very expensive, quite a lot of money would be saved with no reduction in quality. In addition, we must not overlook the inconvenience and discomfort of transporting sick patients from one place to another unnecessarily.

Another problem with all this is that patients have become conditioned to call physicians only during office hours. Sometimes this custom places patients in danger.

Once a new patient called me on a Monday morning and came in to see me that day. Half his face was paralyzed. He had high blood pressure, was overweight, and had circulatory disease. He had all the risk factors for a stroke.

As I talked to him and examined him, it became clear that he had Bell's palsy, a fairly common disease affecting the facial nerve. He did not know that, however, and when I asked him what he thought he had, he told me a stroke. Since his face had started to become paralyzed the previous Thursday, I asked him why he had waited so long to call a doctor. His answer was "I know you cannot get a doctor on a weekend." The poor man had lived with the dreadful belief that he had a stroke for days rather than disturb a doctor.

This can also happen to physicians. On another occasion, a man called me because his teenage son had fallen off his bicycle and landed on his elbow. He called me on a Saturday and asked me if I would see his son on Monday. I told him we needed x-rays now. The x-rays showed a fracture.

I needed an orthopedist to take care of it and the father had a particular one he wanted. It took me 45 minutes to reach him, which is not unusual. Doctors frequently erect barriers to keep patients from disturbing them. I could have reached another orthopedist in five minutes, but they wanted this one. While making all those calls to find him, I could not help thinking that this was one of the reasons the medical profession has lost respect in the eyes of the public.

These problems I mentioned involve the inability of physicians to use medical technology wisely. Used wisely, it is most effective. But physicians are not taught to do that because medical schools have not kept up with the times. They have not changed the training physicians receive in how to decide when to use technology even though the available technology has changed drastically. The broad and important aspects of patient care are still taught in the same way as they were taught when I was a medical student, almost fifty years ago. In fact, they are not taught as well. This is a major part of the problem. Physicians, like most people, do not want to sit by and do nothing when confronted with disease and death. They want to act. Unfortunately, they are not taught well that sometimes restraint must be exercised in the best interests of the patient.

I experienced this sort of tension often. A patient I remember in particular came to me badly jaundiced. At first, I thought he had hepatitis because the jaundice developed very suddenly. I put him in the hospital because he was quite ill, and subsequent studies showed that he had cancer of the pancreas.

With this disease, about all you can do is make the patient more comfortable. To do that, it is sometimes necessary to operate and bypass the obstruction. The cancer closes off the bile duct, and the patient becomes jaundiced and quite uncomfortable. The operation does not extend life, but it makes the patient's remaining life more comfortable.

While performing the operation, the surgeon looked to see if the cancer was operable. They rarely are, but occasionally the surgeon thinks it is and will try. It is somewhat amazing that, despite all our sophisticated technology, problems like this come down to a surgeon looking at a cancerous lump, feeling it, and then deciding what to do. The decision here was that it was an inoperable cancer, the bypass was performed, and three biopsies were made.

Subsequently, I talked to the man and his wife and told them it was cancer and was untreatable. I told them a variety of medicines were being tried, but they all made the patients sick and did not prolong life according to many studies. I advised him not to have any treatment for the cancer, and he and his wife agreed.

Before he left the hospital, the biopsy reports came back and showed normal tissue. According to the surgeon, this happens 40 percent of the time. He remained confident it was cancer.

This is when tensions build in a physician. It is difficult today to do nothing, even when all medical evidence indicates that nothing can be done, that nothing will work. So much of medicine today denies this conclusion or misreads the data to support a more acceptable conclusion. Then we can act.

But nothing could be done for this man. The average life expectancy for disease of this type is about four months. I first diagnosed the disease in March. The patient worked full time after his surgery until November with no medication.

Then I received a plaintive letter from his daughter who lived out of town. She said her father had become depressed and had told his wife that if she talked to me about it he would quit seeing doctors. I answered her letter by saying that if he came in, I would talk to him about it.

When I saw him, he had lost seventy-five pounds, but this did not affect him much since he had been very obese. The cancer was beginning to take its toll symptomatically, however, and he felt quite ill. He had been working up to only a few days before this visit, but it was obvious that he would be unable to continue. Examination showed evidence of an infection, but I was not sure of its nature. He was clearly dying, and there was nothing I could do except, more or less, choose how he would die by deciding on the nature of the subsequent treatment.

I discussed the problem with my partners. The greatest likelihood was that the infection was related to reobstruction of the bile duct and that further surgery may relieve this. However, at this stage of the disease, nothing would make much difference, and I recommended doing nothing. In my own mind, I thought he would be lucky if he died quickly from the infection.

After that visit, he rallied somewhat and returned to my office again. This was a good-bye visit. His whole family was there, and I walked out with my arm around him. He told me how much good I had done him.

As I look back on it, I guess I did do him some good. I will not claim that I gave him eight months of reasonably comfortable, rewarding, satisfying life. *I just did not take it away from him.* He got four months more than the average, and I did not take it away from him by following the impulse to do something—in this instance, to treat his cancer with unproven therapies. At the time, that was a victory.

My years in medicine have taught me that not all medical victories involve curing a patient or preventing death. Often, it involves using your knowledge to make a patient's lot as comfortable as possible. In a sense, this knowledge is what is being lost today and what is leading us to bankruptcy. Medical technology has clouded our vision.

My professional career has been somewhat different from most physicians because I have worked both as a private practitioner and as a full time professor in a medical school. I had the opportunity to see these problems as they developed in medical schools and as they began to affect the medical community. For the first sixteen years of my career, I was in private practice in St. Paul, Minnesota as a general internist. During that time I dealt with the range of medical problems affecting adults from the common to the unusual. My education had prepared me well for this because medical education in the 1940s emphasized clinical judgement and communication with patients much more than it does today. As interns, we were given quite a lot of responsibility, but our teachers were always available to us when we needed help. They were true scholars and compassionate clinicians, and, although they did research, they never shirked their teaching responsibilities. Because medicine was relatively "low tech" then, they also spent considerable time teaching clinical judgement, which today is called decision making capability.

As a Fellow at the Mayo Clinic, I had similar experiences. While there, I was fortunate to be associated with some of the keenest clinical minds I have ever known. The work was hard, the hours long, and time off was rare and short, partly because during World War II and the years that followed many physicians were in the armed forces. This led to a civilian doctor shortage. However, the teachers tried to help make up for this by increasing their patient care work.

The late forties and early fifties were a satisfying time to be in medicine. Despite the relative lack of effective medical treatments available, a wide range of successful surgery was being done, and non-surgical treatments also had many successes. The relationship between physicians and patients was better than it is today because, without today's laboratory diagnostic capabilities, physicians were forced to rely more on the history of symptoms and physical examination of the patient to make correct diagnoses. They learned to communicate with their patients better than they do today.

The saying at that time (attributed to Sir William Osler) was that if you listened to the patient long enough, the patient would tell you the diagnosis. This is still true although it is now often ignored.

The 1940s were no different from today in the proportion of patients whose symptoms were caused by emotional stress from family or job or health concerns. With this group of patients, physicians were at least as successful as today. There were fewer tests to rely on, so we had to spend more time learning from the patient.

The social side of medicine was mixed at best. There was little health insurance available and none for those over sixty-five. The poor, regardless of age, were forced to use the city and county hospitals, usually teaching centers. The care they received was generally good, but the environment was demeaning. Many, perhaps most, physicians saw many patients in their offices for reduced fees or no fees. This was called "Robin Hood" medicine, where the poor were charged little or nothing, and the more affluent were charged higher fees to cover those expenses. This practice continued at least into the middle 1960s when Medicaid and Medicare became law. It is still being done today, but it is much more limited.

In 1966, I left private practice to join the full time faculty at the University of Minnesota Medical School. I made this change because I felt being on the faculty of a medical school would give me a better platform to develop and expand my views of the importance of providing additional facets of education for primary physicians.

Even then, it was becoming apparent that technological solutions to medical problems were being emphasized to a greater extent than before. There was money, prestige, and glamour for physicians pioneering in the various new specialties. Students were deeply affected by these role models, and many chose to follow them into highly technological specialties. This trend has escalated since then.

The inevitable result was that teaching of broad clinical skills deteriorated, and the introduction of what was then a new discipline (for medicine), decision logic, never got off the ground. Clinical judgement suffered because it was not taught effectively. *This is a major cause of many of the problems that we face today.*

To counter this trend, I helped develop the Department of Family Practice and Community Health at the University of Minnesota. This was the first such department in the United States and the second on the North American continent. I was its first professor and head. Later, I moved to the Department of Medicine and helped develop its first Section of Primary Care to educate general internists in broad clinical skills. This was a sharp contrast to the narrow subspecialty programs in internal medicine that were also developing at the time. In both of these departments, I initiated programs I thought were important to the function of primary practitioners in their managerial role in patient care.

These programs were not popular with many of the faculty of the medical school, so after enduring twelve years of battles as a full-time faculty member, I returned to my first love, the private practice of general internal medicine in the community. I also continued teaching part time.

I experienced a great shock upon returning to private practice. Although I knew things had changed in the community while I was teaching, the extent of the change was overwhelming. In the early sixties, there was optimism and satisfaction among physicians. In the late seventies, morale was dropping. While fees had increased considerably, overhead had increased even more. Relationships with hospitals and insurance companies were becoming ever more adversarial. And Medicare, with its many regulations, was a new experience for me.

In retrospect, however, 1977 was not too bad. It has been downhill ever since. I retired in 1989 with mixed feelings, relieved to be free of some of the hassles but missing the contact with patients.

What happened? During all those years, physicians were taught, either directly or by the example of their role models, to intervene. They were taught to use the many new procedures of the subspecialties despite the fact that sound medical reasoning often argued against their use. The miracle of high technology became the best argument for its use in all cases. The clinical skills once thought necessary to guide its use were slowly eroded and devalued.

As the newer developments reached general usage, costs rose exponentially (especially since 1966 when the federal and state governments became insurers). Many of the new developments reached general usage without having proper studies made to determine the efficacy of the products. This began the escalation which led to our fiscal problems today. Currently, it is common to see $1000 per day hospitalization charges and not unusual to see total hospital bills of $250,000 to $500,000.

So there is a problem. Everyone agrees to that. There is less agreement on what to do about it. *There is even less agreement and much confusion as to what is causing the problem.*

Most of the proposals suggested so far to correct this try to control costs through payment mechanisms or try to control physician behavior by fiat. The factor that is rarely addressed adequately is the need for better and newer kinds of education for physicians practicing today. Current medical practice is much more complex than it was even twenty years ago. *Failure of medical educators to modify the curriculum to prepare physicians for their new and different responsibilities has been an appalling oversight (to put it in the kindest possible terms).* Sometimes the term, "educational malpractice" goes through my mind. *This is the disease causing our problems.*

Decisions to use sophisticated and sometimes invasive medical technology are being made almost solely by those who have been trained to use that technology. Education of physicians to make wise decisions about when to use it is no longer considered very important. Bad medicine is the result.

So it should come as no surprise that the complaints of overuse of medical technology increase. Patients suffer more and more from deficient medical decision making in a time of truly miraculous medical progress.

Abraham Maslow probably summed it up best when he said, "If the only tool you have is a hammer, everything looks like a nail."

Chapter Four

IF THE ONLY TOOL YOU HAVE IS A HAMMER, EVERYTHING LOOKS LIKE A NAIL

I look back on my years of practice with both wonderment and sadness. Wonderment because I have been fortunate to have lived and worked in such dynamic times in medicine, and it has been satisfying. And sadness because I am afraid that physicians who are just starting their careers will not realize the tremendous satisfaction and pleasure of being allowed to use their full talents in patient care. This will be more than a loss to individual physicians because, quite possibly, it will mean that the medical profession will no longer be able to fulfill public needs. The "Golden Age" in medicine is passing, and the effects will be devastating.

How devastating? Some years ago, I was asked to see an elderly woman in consultation whose immediate medical problem was due to a circulatory disease. The circulation to both legs was severely impaired, and gangrene was developing in both feet. In addition, she had been confined to a wheelchair for several years because of severe arthritis.

I was asked for an opinion concerning whether I thought surgery might restore the flow of blood to her legs and feet. After examining her and reviewing the data on her chart, I came to the following conclusions:

1. The likelihood of surgically restoring the circulation was small.

2. Her general condition would confine her to a wheelchair for the rest of her life, even if the surgery were successful.

3. Attempting to restore circulation surgically in such severely impaired extremities frequently leads to multiple surgical procedures.

4. The potential benefit to this patient, even with surgical success, was small, and the potential risk of complications with prolonged hospitalization or death was great.

Therefore, I recommended immediate amputation of both legs, one above the knee and one below the knee.

Several days later, I was asked to see the patient again. An arteriogram (an x-ray to show the extent of the circulatory disease) had been done and showed that the circulatory disease in one leg was uncorrectable. It also showed advanced and probably uncorrectable disease in the other leg. However, it introduced slight doubt about immediate amputation by suggesting to some of the observers that there was a remote possibility that surgery might improve circulation in one leg by a small amount. I continued to recommend amputation of both legs as the initial procedure.

On the basis of this x-ray, the physicians in charge decided to amputate one leg and try to surgically repair the circulation in the other leg.

The decision was not made lightly. It followed a conference that lasted an hour and a half which was attended by all of the physicians involved. The above two positions were argued before the final decision was made.

The result was that the patient was in the hospital for four and a half months. She had five surgical procedures and multiple medical complications. In the end, both legs were amputated, one above the knee and one below the knee. She was discharged to nursing home care, totally demoralized.

What went wrong? In a way, nothing. This happened in a prestigious medical center, and all the attending physicians were highly skilled in what they did. They were only doing what they were trained to do. We should not be surprised that physicians trained in a high tech skill seek solutions through using that skill. "If the only tool you have is a hammer, everything looks like a nail."

The public is correct in being frightened by the misuse or abuse of these vast powers. No where is this more apparent than in the desire of many patients to control the abuse of medical technology on the death bed through the use of living wills. If the public thought medical resources were always used rationally, there would not be such a push to keep these resources away from them when they are helpless.

Even people in the health care professions are frightened. A patient of mine—an experienced health professional with frequent exposure to intensive care units—developed a blood clotting disorder. His blood was clotting too much. Clots had formed in his legs and in the arteries of his heart, and he finally had a stroke because of the clotting. The stroke was quite severe, causing paralysis and impairing his ability to think clearly. I told the family there was little that could be done and that he probably had a malignancy—this is often the reason for such clotting—but that we could not locate the cancer.

His condition progressively worsened and it was becoming clear that he would soon be transferred to an intensive care unit where heroic measures would be taken in a futile attempt to get him through these crises. His family said he would not want that. Many times he had returned home from work and had told them that he did not want to end up in one of those units if his condition was hopeless.

So I put a "Do Not Resuscitate" order on his chart with the agreement of his entire family.

Another physician then saw the patient and wrote that he thought the patient was competent to make this decision. I was left with no choice but to try to talk with the patient to see if I could determine his wishes.

I explained his condition to him and then asked him if he wanted aggressive treatment or not should he suddenly worsen. He opened his eyes and mumbled something that sounded like, "Go for broke."

That was all he said. The nurse and I were not sure if he understood what we told him or if we understood what he was saying, but I felt I had to remove the DNR order from his chart.

This happened early in the morning before his wife arrived at the hospital. I left for my office and was paged in my car. It was the patient's wife and she said the DNR order had to be put back on the chart. She was extremely upset because she knew what could happen to him in intensive care. She felt death preferable to the possibility of weeks or months of life in a vegetative state before he died.

I told her that we could not replace the DNR order in view of the new circumstances because if we did so unilaterally it could be viewed as homicide. I returned to the hospital and talked to her and her family again.

We then talked with the lawyer for the hospital. In view of the fact that there was just one dissenting opinion regarding the patient's competence, we elected to go to the probate court to have his wife appointed guardian. The matter was becoming ever more urgent, since he was at high risk of a pulmonary embolism (a blood clot to the lung) and a cardiac arrest.

Fortunately, things moved quickly. The probate court granted her a partial guardianship after hearing the testimony. This meant that she could authorize a DNR order, but she could not authorize removing him from artificial life support if he were already on it.

She got back to the hospital in time to authorize the order. He died shortly after this was done. An autopsy revealed a large pulmonary embolism and an inoperable cancer.

Much has been written recently about the problems of the health professions by both physicians and non-physicians. But, unfortunately, most of the physicians writing on these subjects are not in community practice. They are based in institutions like medical schools which seriously limits their experience in day-to-day patient care. They function in a fairly restricted environment of research medicine and primarily treat patients who have unusual conditions. One study, for example, showed that in a typical population, 72 percent visit a physician in a clinic at least once a year, 10 percent are admitted to a hospital at least once a year, and only 1 percent are admitted to a university hospital once a year.[1] In recent years even fewer patients have been admitted to hospitals. This certainly suggests that medical students' education is not based on the overall needs of the public.

This is a *crucial* part of the part of the problem because academic physicians control the educational system. *Medical students and residents are taught medicine based almost solely on the needs of this small, unrepresentative segment of the total population.* It's a vicious circle, because the medical needs of this small segment of the population are generally "high tech." The result has been the explosion of "high tech" medicine practiced relatively indiscriminately on the population at large despite the flaws in its scientific evaluation and flaws in the decision-making process determining its use. Examples of this are legion and are reported with great regularity in the medical journals and mass media. One example is the overuse of invasive x-ray techniques. Other examples recently studied include coronary artery bypass surgery and hysterectomies. Often, a careful discussion of the patient's symptoms and a good physical examination would give the same information as the test and make the test or treatment unnecessary. All at a saving of time, money, and risk.

For several decades, the drama associated with medical technology—life support systems, transplants, laser surgery, etc.—has led many physicians as well as the public to believe that technology is the essence of medical practice. This has led to the domination of the technological side of patient care over the conceptual side.

For example, in teaching centers the idea prevails that there are two sciences—hard science (technological) and soft science (conceptual). Hard science in this paradigm is the "good" science and soft science the "mushy" science. Hard science is associated with all the advances in surgery, medical imagery, drug therapy, etc. Soft science, on the other

---

[1] Kerr L. White, Life and Death in Medicine, *Scientific American,* Sept., 1973, Vol 229, pp. 23–33.

hand, is associated with such disciplines as the study of medical decision making, communication skills, and human behavior.

Obviously, both of these components of medical education are important. Without knowing the current facts relating to medical practice, physicians could not practice medicine effectively, nor would the public recognize them as physicians. This knowledge is integral to being a physician.

But is that knowledge enough for a physician in today's high tech. environment?

What is interesting is that what are considered by technologists to be "hard facts" are actually quite mushy. This is born out by the observation that the half life of medical knowledge today is less than five years. This means that half of the so called "hard" data learned in medical schools are out of date and wrong within five years. Medical school graduates relying on those data would rapidly become incompetent if they did not forget the old "facts" and learn all the new "hard" data.

But the "soft sciences," the broad concepts in patient care, are largely eternal, and a well rounded physician knows and understands these truths. They are the bases for making sound medical decisions in an uncertain and ever changing environment and for understanding human behavior and its effects on health and communication.

For instance, in taking a medical history, a physician must understand that a patient's age, background, outlook, anxieties, and religion are a few of the variables that influence how patients describe their problems to a physician.

I once saw a patient whose bile duct was partially obstructed with a stone, and an infection was developing in the duct and going up into the liver. This is a serious problem in any patient but was particularly serious in this patient because she was elderly and a diabetic.

During the medical interview, before we knew what her problem was, she said only once that she felt a little pain. I knew it was part of her view of life to attach little importance to pain or disability since she was sustained by a great religious faith. It was important to know the intensity of this pain, however, because surgical exploration of her abdomen was the issue.

When I asked her about it, she said she was unable to describe it. So I asked her if it was just an awareness, an annoyance, or a severe pain. She said it was an annoyance.

This still was not very helpful, because annoyance could be as insignificant as a bump on the shin. So I asked her if there was anything in her life to which she could compare this annoyance.

She said, "It is more annoying than were the births of my children."

That statement was instrumental in my decision to proceed with the examinations which led to an extensive operation.

In this instance, it was knowledge of the "mushy" sciences that led to the correct diagnosis. Yet, the hard sciences dominate medical education so totally that medical students are primarily taught how to accumulate multiple and often isolated facts with little emphasis on their use and with little understanding of their meaning. Implicit in this system is the belief that if something is available, it should be used.

In today's health care system, primary physicians—those who should be educated to perform an overall managerial role—are instead losing their authority in the educational structure and their visibility to the public. This is reflected in many ways, but especially in the recent categorization of them as "gatekeepers" of the system. This term suggests that their main function is to keep as many people out as possible and to function as referral agents for the rest. Not only does this designation fail to recognize their important managerial role, it is also an extremely pejorative term which does little to bolster their self-esteem or their enthusiasm for their role in patient care. Their loss of stature within the profession is also reflected by their relatively small incomes as compared to the technological group of physicians.

This leads to the overuse of medical resources. Not only does this not help patients, but it places them at considerable risk. I do not minimize the importance of accumulating medical facts nor do I minimize the wonders of modern technology. But let us also not minimize the importance of the conceptual side of medicine.

Chapter Five

THE FOURTH REVOLUTION

Today's problems in patient care come as no surprise. They were easily predictable since the 1950s. Actually, they should have been predictable since the 1930s although not as easily. As a matter of fact, the earlier reforms in medical education which were fought for since the late 1800s and which were implemented in 1910 by the issuance of the Flexner Report really set the scene for what is happening now. Flexner did not intend for it to happen this way. He even placed a strong caveat in his report to avoid it, but his advice was either ignored or not understood.

My generation of physicians has lived through most of these changes during our professional lifetime, since they really started after the end of World War II. It took that long for the changes effected by the Flexner Report to have an impact.

This is what happened.

There have been four revolutions in the medical profession this century, sweeping changes that make a large difference throughout a system. They change the quality of life — for better or for worse.

The first was educational. Although it really started shortly after the Civil War and was supported by such eminent physicians as Sir William Osler as early as the 1880s, it was not implemented until the Carnegie Foundation commissioned Abraham Flexner, an educator (not a physician), to personally examine all of the medical schools in the United States and Canada. He found the condition of most of them to be deplorable and issued his report in 1910. He confirmed that most medical schools of that day were extremely ill equipped. They had virtually no laboratories or education in basic sciences. The teaching was inadequate. Many of the students had not even graduated from high school. He concluded that the public was being poorly served by large numbers of physicians who were ignorant of science. He recommended extensive reforms including defined requirements for education in the basic sciences, education in clinical medicine, and for admission to medical schools. He also recommended that medical schools be affiliated with universities.

His report resulted in the closing of many schools and the affiliation of many others with universities. The quality of medical education improved substantially. It was probably this revolution which made possible many of the brilliant advances which have occurred since World War II.

It is interesting that Henry S. Pritchett, who was president of the Carnegie Foundation, stated in the introduction that the recommendations made in the report were conditioned on three factors: *"first, upon the creation of a public opinion which shall discriminate between the ill-trained and rightly-trained physician,* and which will also insist upon the enactment of such laws as will require all practitioners of medicine, whether they belong to one sect or another, to ground themselves in the fundamentals upon which medical science rests; second, *upon the universities and their attitude towards medical standards and medical support,* and, finally, *upon the attitude of the members of the medical profession towards the standards of their own practice and upon their sense of honor with respect to their own profession."*[1]

It seems to me that the changes called for in this book are conditioned on the same three factors.

The second revolution was economic. It started in the 1930s with the advent of health insurance. Before that, patients paid for their health care out of pocket.

This change altered the relationship between the physician and patient in a very fundamental way. Before health insurance, the interaction between the physician and patient had to include the cost factor, which was bound to affect decisions made by both the physician and the patient. Physicians had to consider the relationship of cost and benefit much more carefully and also explain it to the patient in much more detail than at present when an impersonal third party is paying. This altered relationship has had an adverse effect on communication with patients and has led to a tendency to inappropriately overutilize our resources. Patients began to adopt the attitude that the proposed test or treatment was free, and, since it was already covered by insurance, they might as well have it done. Many physicians went along with this charade although they knew better.

As health insurance became more available, both diagnostic and thera-

---

[1] Henry S. Pritchett, The Flexner Report, *Science and Health Publications,* Washington, D.C., p. xlll.

peutic modalities began to be used to an ever greater extent. People were admitted to hospitals more readily, many times for treatments and tests that did not require hospitalizations and many times for treatments or tests they didn't need. More hospitals were built. More duplication of facilities occurred.

The biggest influence on this was the advent of Medicare and Medicaid in 1966. The government became the biggest insurer to two groups which had previously been uninsured, the elderly and the poor. It gave these two large groups access to the entire health care system, something many of them had never enjoyed before. There is no question of the benefits which resulted from this. One negative, however, was the disproportionate increase in aggregate cost, often without benefit to the individual patient and sometimes with harmful results.

The year, 1966, can be readily identified on the graphs depicting increased cost of medical care, even without any dates, since the curve moves exponentially upward from then on.

The third revolution was technologic. I will summarize the unbelievable changes with one example, the redefinition of death. In the 1940s and 1950s (and even part of the 1960s) death was adequately defined as cessation of function of the heart and lungs. This was adequate because the heart and lungs provided the sustenance for all the other organs. Without function of either of these organs, the entire body died. The function of these organs is necessary to maintain brain function, and the brain is necessary to the function of the other vital organs. Consequently, when the heart and/or lungs failed, the brain ceased to function, and when the brain failed, all the other organs ceased to function.

With modern technology, this is no longer true. With artificial life support, all of the vital organs can be artificially maintained in the absence of brain function. In other words, a person can be "brain dead" and still have breathing, heart action, and kidney function maintained artificially. Even fairly adequate nutrition can be provided.

The implications of this are horrendous in terms of human dignity and also in terms of useless expenditures. This is one of the reasons brain death legislation has been enacted in most states.

I use the above example only to show the power of our technology. There is no question that we are potentially better off as a society because of all the advances that have been made than we were fifty years ago. There is also no question that the benefit is dependent on how the technology is utilized for the individual patient.

Examine the sequence of these three revolutions. The educational revolution made medical practice more effective. As this became apparent to the public, they began to use it more extensively. This led to the development of health insurance, initially to help the individual patients fund their care. As the health insurance industry grew, and particularly with the advent of Medicare and Medicaid, larger and larger sums of private and governmental moneys became available to fund research, medical education, and hospital expansion as well as individual patient care. It was a wonderful ride which led to many exciting discoveries. However, now the money is running out unless we do something about it.

The fourth revolution is occurring now. This is the most critical of the four, since it will determine if it is possible to continue to afford medical care without some deliberate and official kind of rationing. It also will determine if we can afford the goal of equal access to all who need care. It also will determine whether we can go to less of a two-tier system of care than we now have or whether it will get worse.

The fourth revolution is a power struggle for control over decision making. The adversaries in the struggle are physicians, patients, administrators in the various insurance plans, hospital administrators, and government agencies.

At the moment it appears to me that the physicians and patients are losing the struggle under the guise of cost control. If this happens, there are grave implications for the future of patient care.

I say grave implications, because the struggle is ill defined as regards the issues that are involved. As of now, the over-riding issue is cost. For this reason, the current battleground is cost control defined by dollar cost alone. The goal is to reduce dollar cost by arbitrarily defining need. Thus far, all attempts have failed. In a recent issue of the *New England Journal of Medicine,* Arnold Relman states "Few observers expect present cost control efforts to be successful. Conventional wisdom holds that unrestrained consumer demand coupled with the relentless development of increasingly sophisticated new technology will keep driving costs up until some major new approach is adopted. The most likely next step, many now believe, will be some form of systematic rationing."[2]

Because of high costs, there is increasing discussion of the need for rationing care. The discussions are sometimes difficult to follow, since

---

[2]Relman, Arnold S., Is Rationing Inevitable? *NEJM,* June 21, 1990, 322:1800.

rationing is defined in many ways. Some say we have it now and have always had it. This is true if you define rationing as withholding treatment because its benefit is too marginal to justify its risk (a good form of rationing), or if you define it as withholding treatment on the basis of inability to pay or inability to obtain health insurance (price rationing), a bad form of rationing. This latter form of rationing must be addressed and eliminated.

But now a new form of rationing is being discussed. This is the withholding of treatment from those who may clearly benefit and have resources (insurance or cash) to pay for it. At present, this is discussed mainly with reference to the older segment of our population. I suppose the older segment is looked at first because they stand to benefit the least insofar as long-term gain is concerned and also because they tend to be higher utilizers of care. I believe that this form of rationing can and should be avoided, not just for the aged but for all segments of the population.

I further believe that properly educated physicians, making clean medical choices, based on risks and benefits, would reduce inappropriate utilization appreciably and significantly reduce total cost. This form of reduction of utilization would not single out any group and, in fact, would benefit everyone. Unneeded procedures help no one and hurt some.

Arbitrary rationing places physicians in an untenable position. It makes them truly "gatekeepers" for the system in the worst sense. *It is antithetical to the most basic values in medicine and would result in a restive and cynical profession at best.* It is almost comparable to requiring physicians to participate in active euthanasia. Physicians fear this, and rightly so. A better and more equitable means of cost control must be found.

We seem to have entered an age of medical decision making heavily influenced by financial managers in governmental and private insurance companies. It is not surprising that all attempts have failed so far, since any attempt at cost control without maintaining or improving quality is destined to fail. And simplistic and arbitrary attempts to define need are bound to reduce quality.

As a matter of fact, cost of patient care has to be viewed as tripartite, including unnecessary death, pain and suffering of patients and families, and dollar cost. I have always maintained that if the first two are controlled, dollar costs will take care of themselves. Avoidance of needless pain and suffering and unnecessary death are two important outcomes denoting high quality. I don't think that anyone would argue that quality and cost are inversely related.

When financial managers apply their knowledge of balance sheets to the care of individual patients, strange things happen. Payments for health care have always been skewed toward tangible forms of care and against the cognitive work required to make a decision. For example, a clerk looking at a computer screen may allow thousands of dollars as payment to a hospital and surgical team for a coronary bypass operation while disallowing the requested payment for a couple of hours of a diagnostician's time who has just determined that a patient's chest pain does not originate in the heart.

In addition to the dollar cost issue, there is another issue of control in the power struggle, and that is control over medical decisions.

Should physicians lose this phase of the struggle, they will lose their professional status and become artisans. Decision making capacity will become unimportant to them because their decisions will be made for them on the basis of preconceived formulae or algorithms. Individualization of patient care will become history.

The dangerous part of this power struggle currently under way is that the issues have not been clarified. The struggle is being conducted on only one level which is cost control (at the moment through managed care techniques) and the issue of professionalism and skillful decision making for patients on an individual basis is being ignored. Should this continue, quality of care will regress and all costs (including dollar cost) will rise.

In summary, I believe that dollar cost control may be a legitimate responsibility of people possessing skills in business methods but that control of decisions relating to individual patients must be the responsibility of properly educated physicians. These issues must be dealt with separately.

Chapter Six

THE "ART" OF MEDICINE

Medical practice is very difficult if done properly. Illness is generally unique to each individual. Rarely is the disease the only determinant of outcome. This is why the care of patients with the same disease might be quite different for each patient, and why decision making must be done with all the variables peculiar to a specific patient in mind. Such variables include the patient's overall physical condition, environment, social and cultural background, etc. They include the way patients relate their health problems to the physician, their attitudes towards pain and illness, how they think, and the state of their emotions. They include the overall life situation of the patients. This is why simple algorithms (standard guidelines for diagnosis and treatment) do not work well and will probably never work well.

Tests are often misused because of the almost mystical belief of many people, including medical educators, that sound medical decision making is part of the "art" of medicine. These people seem to believe that, with experience, practicing physicians will develop a vague "feel" for diagnosing illness and then will follow their hunches to successful and happy conclusions. Some even go so far as to say that, since "art" is such an important part of medical practice, the process of selecting medical students would benefit from dropping some of the science requirements of the premedical curriculum. This idea has been bandied about for a number of years.

Proponents of the idea suggest that too much emphasis is placed on scientific achievement and not enough on humanistic qualities in the criteria that have been developed to aid in selecting a medical school class. Thus, some of the science prerequisites for entrance into medical school have been dropped. The thought behind these changes is that requiring less scientific background for medical students would somehow produce a more compassionate and understanding physician.

But that ignores the realities that practicing physicians face every day. Individual patients bring problems unique to them that are best resolved by application of rigorous decision making logic after acquiring maximum relevant information from the patient relating to both medical and behavioral data. This is a far cry from invoking the vague concept of an "art."

I suspect that one of the main reasons the "art of medicine" continues to be discussed is because of the old shibboleth so prevalent among medical educators that these things can't be taught. The saying goes that students either have these skills or don't have them when they come to medical school. This implies that some people are born with the skills and others are not. Of course, this is patent nonsense. There is no such thing as the "art of medicine." The term was coined long ago before sciences dealing with communication, decision logic, and human behavior had developed. But today these fields are well developed and highly teachable.

To invoke the art of medicine as an excuse not to teach these things is like calling the world flat because we cannot usually see the curvature.

For instance, an eighteen year old woman came to see me with a temperature of 104 degrees. She was in great pain, which she did not disclose at the time of making the appointment, and so she was scheduled for only thirty minutes. The question finally worked down to whether she had acute appendicitis or a tubal pregnancy. The interaction ended up taking an hour and a half.

Her symptoms were not typical for appendicitis, and this complicated the problem. I asked her if there was any chance she might be pregnant. She said yes, and she made it clear that she did not want her parents, who were in the waiting room, to know that. She wanted me to tell them only if it were highly probable, preoperatively, that it was a tubal pregnancy. After further examination, I decided that it was not a tubal pregnancy. Because of the unusually high fever and a very high white blood count, I thought the appendix had already ruptured. This is what I told her parents.

At surgery, she had appendicitis. The appendix had not ruptured. The high fever and white blood count were unexplained.

I did not arrive at that diagnosis because of hunches or vague feelings. It was hard and time consuming work.

There is little question that communication is often the weakest part of the physician-patient relationship. This is strange, because the communication between the two is what starts the physician on a rational course of diagnosis and treatment. I am not talking about an "art" here, but about a teachable skill which at present is inadequately taught. Those who call it an art are making it into a kind of "mushy" process and regard it in the same way that they regard the sociological side of patient care.

This is why attempts to recruit medical students with less scientific background and more of a "humanitarian" background sidesteps the whole problem. To believe that this will somehow improve the clinical skills of the students is flawed. The problem is not, and never has been, the type of people choosing medical careers. The problem is in the medical education they receive.

The obvious fallacy in such thinking is that these suggestions ignore the profound influence medical education has on its students. Not only do they learn the scientific aspects of disease, but they are intensely socialized into the profession. The socialization of the medical student is an extremely significant process. When they start medical school, they are generally young, malleable, easily influenced by their experiences, and frightened. It is not surprising that the medical school socializing process has at least as much and maybe more lasting impact on the students as their scientific education, and it can be either good or bad. As it now exists, it tends to reinforce many of the attitudes and practices that lead to the overuse of medical technology.

Are entering medical students any different today as compared to forty or fifty years ago? This is a question I am often asked. Are they different kinds of people? Are they motivated differently? Are they less compassionate than students of previous years? Are they more likely to be financially motivated in their career selection? These are complex, judgmental questions which are not easy to answer. An answer requires that we consider the profound influence of the medical school culture on the student as well as the influence of technological development on medical education and medical practice since the end of World War II.

Because medical school is a very intense experience, and because medicine can be a harrowing and lonely profession, medical students have always undergone profound socialization. The medical profession used to be called a "fraternity," and physicians used to relate to each other more than to those outside of the profession. At their parties, most of the guests were physicians, and the conversation was largely "shop talk." This helped blunt the responsibility and ease the loneliness.

When I was a medical student, we spent a large portion of our first six months dissecting a cadaver. Two students shared one cadaver. By the third year, we were working in hospitals seeing many critically ill patients.

It was a different life from those studying in other colleges and made powerful images on a developing mind.

Today, those images may be even more powerful, since fewer young people today have experienced or seen closely serious illness, nor have many of them had anyone close to them die. Experiencing this for the first time can be very unsettling.

Added to that is the mystique surrounding high tech. medicine. Not only does it give physicians an aura of power, but those who teach this side of medicine tend to have more status. This is not lost on students. They learn from their teachers and role models what their professional lives should be like.

Even in the sixties, this was a problem. Back then, I had the responsibility for arranging a series of lectures for first year medical students. The series covered a broad range of topics relating to the social aspects of medicine as practiced in the community. One of the speakers I invited was a sociologist, nationally known and respected for his studies on American attitudes toward death.

He gave a short lecture and then presented a film that dramatized one man's death. The point of the film was to acquaint the students with how our society tends to try to deny death. The main character in the film was an elderly man in a nursing home whose life was presented in a series of flashbacks. It was a typical life in all respects. He was a blue collar worker who had always worked hard and enjoyed the life he lived. Then he died, and the film showed his body being removed from his room almost surreptitiously and taken from the nursing home in an unmarked station wagon. It was almost as if he had never lived there.

When the film was over, the sociologist asked the class what they had seen, and a woman in the back of the lecture room said, "A shitty little death."

The sociologist said, "Yes, that is right. That's why I showed it. But why was it a shitty little death?"

From the other back corner of the room came the reply, "Because it was a shitty little life."

That floored the lecturer. He didn't know what to say. Later, students complained to me about this course, saying they did not think they could learn anything of value from non-physicians. Remember, these were students early in their first year of medical school and not yet fully socialized into the profession. But they had already picked up some strong attitudes, namely that medicine is a hard science above all else.

At the University of Minnesota, my class (1945) became the first class where over fifty percent of the students chose to enter specialty fields. The military assignment system was the major influence on these decisions, because the more specialized the physicians were, the better their duty assignments would be in the military, and we all expected to be called to active duty upon graduation.

But specialty training was different then. Most internists and pediatricians, trained in specialty fields, would be considered generalists by today's standards. Even surgical training, with few exceptions, was quite general. In fact, this type of specialized training probably was a boost to overall educational quality at that time.

Today, however, the numbers of students selecting highly technological and specialized fields has greatly increased and exceeded the need. The significance of this exceeds the raw numbers, because most specialties are now so complex and technological that those practicing them cannot also practice general, primary care medicine. They must limit their practice to their specialty in order to remain proficient in it. This means that most specialists today cannot make difficult medical decisions outside their specialty.

Medical schools have changed drastically over the past fifty years to keep abreast of these technologic changes. They have expanded their disease oriented curriculum and have changed the internal organization of departments and the overall medical school structure.

These are the very changes that have influenced medical students so profoundly. They see the attitudes of their teachers, and they see who has power and status in the medical community. This determines their choice of role models which in turn affects their attitudes toward medical practice. It begins when they are in medical school and continues through their residency training.

I saw this again and again when I led seminars for residents. By the time they are in their residency programs, the socialization is almost complete for most of them. I have taught medical residents all of my professional life, even when I was in private practice, and they are a very bright and talented group. When I taught them about specific disease medicine, they were always interested and attentive.

However, when I led into discussions of the limitations of what they had learned and the need for learning how to evaluate new knowledge in the context of risk and benefit for the patient, most became very threatened and defensive. They inferred that I was telling them that their past eight years had been wasted, and this was a difficult barrier to overcome. I failed to overcome it with many of them. It seemed to be too late to introduce new ideas, subjecting what they had already learned to strict, logical analysis.

I will give two examples of what I mean.

The first related to discussions of limitations of new techniques. I would point out to them that procedures such as angiography and coronary artery bypass surgery were being done more than was necessary or indicated. I pointed out that autopsy studies on healthy young soldiers killed in Korea showed extensive lesions that would have been apparent had angiography been done on them; much more extensive than anyone had ever suspected would be present in a representative sample of apparently healthy young men.

Yet, when angiography is done on patients and shows similar lesions, the first impulse is to operate. I would ask the residents if this was clearly of benefit to many of these patients. Sometimes it would be, depending on other factors, but what was obvious from the discussions was that they had not been taught explicitly to seek out the other factors and determine a risk/benefit ratio independent of the arteriographic findings.

The other example that stood out was their unwillingness to accept that there was much they could learn about how to get more accurate information from patients by developing better interviewing skills. Their attitude was "I have been talking to people all my life. What more can I be taught?" Students disliked having their medical interviews videotaped. Many seemed to believe that a questionnaire or a computer program was all that was necessary to obtain adequate information.

In modern medical education, all of the socializing influence of medical school is toward high technology and narrow specialization. Academic centers have failed to recognize the importance of role models in primary care areas to medical students. Physicians interested in developing primary care programs have been discouraged from being faculty members. Thus, the predominant role models are the researchers and the technologically oriented specialists. The academic community failed to recognize that the absence of role models in the primary care specialties would cause these specialties to wither.

And wither they did.

In addition to not providing the role models, the academic centers also failed to provide additions to the curriculum content of primary care to make the field manageable to its practitioners. If the role models had been present, the curricular additions would undoubtedly have been made.

In the face of all these changes, are the entering medical students any different from those of the past regarding motivation in seeking a medical career? I don't think so. I believe they were well motivated then and are well motivated now when they begin their medical education.

Are they different when they finish their education? I believe that most of them are because the medical education process has changed their attitudes materially. Medical education (as any type of education) influences and changes its students. If it didn't, it wouldn't be education. My point is that it is not change that is important, but the direction of the change and the reasons for it.

The implications of this are serious to the future of patient care.

Chapter Seven

NEEDED: LOGICAL PROBLEM SOLVING SKILLS

Medical practice is rewarding in many ways. Physicians are generally respected by the public. They still have more autonomy in the day to day conduct of their work than most people. Their financial security is generally assured.

The public is familiar with this side of it.

Medical practice is lonely. It can be highly stressful, both emotionally and physically. It is sometimes terrifying.

This is the side of it not usually seen by the public.

This dichotomy has been present through all of my professional life, but it has been changing steadily throughout the years of my practice. The rewards are fewer and the less desirable aspects are increasing.

Although it seems paradoxical, I relate these negative changes largely to the brilliant advances in medical science that have occurred since World War II. The advances did not cause the changes directly, but they created situations in medical practice with which few physicians could cope. The changes in medical technology led to more choices for diagnosing and treating. Physicians today not only have to decide what to do in each patient encounter but also what not to do. *Many more decisions today must be made about what not to do—what tests not to use, what treatments not to follow—than ever before. And deciding not to do something is much more difficult.*

Patient care is basically an exercise in logical thinking. It is now and always has been if done properly.

The major problem faced today in patient care is that medical students, although well taught about diseases, tests, and treatments, are not taught well about people or about thinking analytically. Our highly technological environment requires better teaching of analytical skills, communication skills, and certain aspects of medical sociology than was needed thirty or forty years ago, but this is not happening.

So we have a situation where decisions are often seemingly absurd, and patients and their families are left feeling like victims who are somehow to blame for their problems.

For example, I received a phone call the other day from the wife of a former patient of mine. Since I am retired, she knew I could not participate actively in resolving the problem, but she wanted advice in deciding how to best help her husband. He had developed a widespread and very virulent cancer and had been in and out of the hospital (mostly in) for about two months. There was no cure for this kind of cancer. The only treatment left was to control pain and provide comfort as he died.

Because of strictures on staying in hospitals put in place by most insurance companies, including Medicare, he had been sent home from the hospital several times although it was not possible to control his pain at home with the resources available there. This had been demonstrated several times, and he always ended up back in the hospital for more intensive pain medication.

His wife had resolved the problem of his imminent death pretty well. What she was asking me about was how to deal with the problem of going from home to hospital repeatedly for pain control. She had explored the question of hospice care (where comfort and pain control could be provided outside of the acute care hospital setting), and had discussed it with her husband. Both favored this approach. Her problem was that her husband's physician would not sign the order for hospice care because he did not view the patient as "terminal." He agreed that there was no cure available and that the patient was going to die of the illness, but would not send him to a hospice until there was definite evidence of vital organ involvement.

The wife was quite distraught and, needless to say, bitter. That is why she was asking me for help. *She said that, at times, she almost felt she and her husband were victims of a conspiracy of the medical profession.* How else could one explain this series of irrational, even absurd medical decisions that made it so difficult for a dying man to get consistently effective pain control?

After a fairly prolonged discussion, we decided that the best course would be to obtain a second opinion from someone eminent in the medical community. To keep it as neutral as possible, we decided to call someone from a different city. I made it clear that the consultant may agree with the attending physician and the wife understood this. On the other hand, if the consultant agreed with the patient and his wife, he was prepared to sign the order for transfer to a hospice.

The patient and his wife then reviewed the situation again with the attending physician who remained unmoved. Although he agreed the patient would die, he said sending him to hospice care would be like "putting him out to pasture," and he refused to do it.

Subsequently, the wife talked with the hospital administrators and asked them to arrange temporary staff privileges for the consultant. The purpose of the consultation was explained to them, and they arranged for staff privileges after inquiring into the credentials of the consultant. All of this took several days.

The afternoon before the consultant was to come, a meeting occurred between the attending physician, the hospital administration, and, I presume, members of the executive committee of the medical staff. Following this meeting, the attending physician signed the transfer order. The consultant never needed to come.

This is a dramatic example of a problem that occurs very frequently. Sometimes it is even more dramatic, but sometimes it only involves ordering an extra test or prescribing an additional treatment.

Obviously, something was very wrong with this whole situation. At no time was there any question of anyone's knowledge of medicine. The only question really was why was the medical profession seemingly an adversary of this patient? Why were such bad decisions made?

What does this mean? What are its implications concerning patient care in our high technology environment?

I think the meaning is quite clear. I believe the medical profession is remiss in not assuming greater responsibility for its behavior and insisting that more rationality be exhibited in decision making. We are failing in this responsibility for many reasons that have been discussed in this book, but I want to discuss one of them now because it relates directly to the question of logical thinking.

Many patient care decisions are made in the face of dilemmas. A dilemma is a problem with no satisfactory solution. However, often one solution is less unsatisfactory than others. When this happens, a decision must be made if good patient care is to be achieved even though none of the outcomes are desirable. When decisions are not made, the outcome is almost always worse.

When dilemmas occur in patient care, there is an overwhelming tendency to call them "moral dilemmas." I suppose this is because the stakes are often very high, usually relating to increased pain and suffering or death of a fellow human being.

I submit that dilemmas in patient care are not moral dilemmas most of the time. Most of the time, they are "medical dilemmas." By that, I mean that their resolution can be determined most satisfactorily for the patient based on the biomedical data. If the data have been carefully accumulated and analyzed, a decision can be made about what to do based on whether the proposed procedure is likely to work. Is it likely to benefit the patient? If it will work, do it. If not, don't.

The problem comes when medical dilemmas are confused with moral dilemmas. Moral dilemmas can only be resolved by invoking value judgements and are exceedingly difficult of resolution. When this happens, the decision makers (usually the physicians) decide not to impose their value judgements on the patient and decide to do something (give the "benefit of the doubt" to the patient) despite the improbability of success. I believe this is illogical and that it leads to much inappropriate overutilization of resources.

Much pain and suffering and needless expense could be avoided if the distinction between medical and moral dilemmas were better understood.

This does not mean that medical dilemmas are always easy of resolution. Frequently, they are not. It does mean, however, that there is a clean, decisive pathway to follow in order to resolve them. On the other hand, because moral dilemmas invoke value judgements, there is no decisive way to resolve them.

It is fortunate that most dilemmas in patient care are medical dilemmas. It only remains to begin to teach the distinction to the medical profession.

The implications of these deficits in patient care in our high technology environment are also very clear. If they are not recognized as serious deficits and corrected, we will simply see more of the same. We will see it at an ever accelerating rate since our technology will continue to expand. Quality of care will continue to fall, costs will continue to rise, and access to care will become ever more limited to larger segments of the population. Rationing of care will be inevitable.

The body of knowledge for teaching these skills to those physicians who need to have them is readily available and has been available for at least the past twenty years.

All that needs to be done now is to get the teaching programs organized and implemented.

Chapter Eight

TOO MANY COOKS...

Who is in charge when a patient undergoes any complex or long-term treatment? No one, because, in a sense, just about everyone is—that is the problem. Each physician involved stakes out an area of expertise, a part of the patient's body that other physicians are expected to stay out of.

The thought that medical education should provide one physician who is able to manage the patient's overall treatment remains more or less an idealized vision; to some observers, perhaps, it is even an anachronism. Such a physician is thought of as a Marcus Welby type, the old general practitioner who knew all his patients' names and backgrounds and always made certain that they received the best care no matter how many specialists were called in to help. That is the myth that prevails.

The reality is that we now have a patient care system dominated and ruled by technologists. Their power remains unchallenged from the medical school hierarchy to the practicing community. Such a setting leads to increased use of tests and treatments which often will not help the patient.

So, the question becomes who *should* be in charge. And, at times, it *should* be the physicians in narrow, high tech specialties. For instance, when they are called specifically to perform a certain procedure, they should have the authority to do it in accord with their expertise in that area. Their authority should be limited to that procedure. This is called a limited referral.

However, much of the time, particularly in the care of the elderly and of patients with chronic disability in all age groups, it is not so simple. The question then becomes not just doing the procedure, *but whether it should be done at all,* and, if so, which of a variety of alternatives would best suit a particular patient's needs. In these complex situations, the physician responsible for the decision should be a physician with a breadth of knowledge concerning the patient's limitations, other risk factors relating to that patient, and how much benefit would accrue to the patient given his or her other disabilities.

This is superior to having no one in charge or the wrong physician in charge. A good manager is always superior to decisions by committee. Committees can give good advice, but the final decisions must be made by one responsible physician who is capable of synthesizing all of the advice.

An example of the first instance when no one appears to be in charge occurs most often in seriously ill or critically ill patients with multiple problems in several organ systems. These patients are usually in critical care areas of the hospital and are often post-operative patients. They usually have several physicians seeing them, generally a specialist for each organ system. In addition, there may be a surgeon as well. When this happens there is danger that no one will be responsible for the total care of that patient. *Often, no one will even know who is in overall charge.* I have seen many instances where patients did not know who their doctor was, the nurses did not know whom to call with specific questions, and sometimes even the physicians did not know who had ultimate responsibility for decisions. When this happens, decisions do not get made at all or bad decisions are made.

Examples of the wrong kind of physician being in charge can occur in a variety of settings. One example that comes to mind is an elderly patient of mine who had cancer of the prostate gland. It had been present for many years and he was receiving maximum treatment for it. He had been seen by several of the leading specialists in our state for this problem. In addition, he also had a small aortic aneurysm, too small, in my opinion, to warrant an operation in view of his general condition.

His major symptom was mild incontinence of urine because of the prostatic cancer. None of the physicians who had seen him felt surgery was indicated for the problem.

He ultimately decided to see another urologist. There is nothing wrong with that. All patients have the right to further opinion. The problem was that the new urologist made his decisions without consulting the previous doctors for details of the past.

The result was that the patient had two major operations, one on the prostate gland and one on the small aneurysm which the new physician thought had just been discovered. Had I been consulted, I would have advised against both surgeries. The prostatic cancer was already controlled and the risk of the aneurysm surgery far outweighed any possible benefit to the patient.

The next time I saw the patient, he was demoralized and bitter. He was much more severely incontinent than he had been before the prostatic operation. He had really never understood the operation on his aorta at all. He remained severely incontinent until his death.

His problems all stemmed, of course, from the fact that he had no overall manager for his care in the institution where his two surgeries occurred. One highly specialized physician took control of his treatment without considering other problems the patient might have and without working with a generalist physician to assure that the patient's needs were met.

One reason for the confusion over the years was that the term "primary physician" is not clearly understood. It is somehow equated with a physician who deals only with the simple problems of patient care and refers everything else. This is not what the Millis Commission, which coined the term, had in mind. In fact, John Millis lectured on this subject repeatedly in the years following publication of the report. He was disappointed in the misunderstanding of the term and said again and again the physician he was urging be educated would be a knowledgeable and capable physician meant to be *in charge of the overall care of the patient.* A friend of mine suggests that the term "principal physician" would more accurately describe the function of primary physicians.

As the influence of the primary physicians declined, the job description of physicians became ever more blurred. In 1971, Rosemary Stevens, a leading scholar in hospital administration and health care asked, "What, indeed, is a physician?" and then concluded *"And this question is as yet unanswered."*[1] (emphasis added)

It remains unanswered in 1994.

From the public's point of view, there should be only two types of physicians. I proposed in 1978 that they be called conceptually oriented physicians and technologically oriented physicians.[2] They are also sometimes called cognitive physicians and procedural physicians. The technologically oriented physicians embrace most of the subspecialties and their functions are well understood. This is because their specialty

---

[1] Rosemary Stevens, *American Medicine and the Public Interest,* Yale University Press, New Haven, Connecticut, 1971, p. 531.
[2] Fuller & Fuller, *Physician or Magician?*, McGraw Hill, 1978, p. 33.

defines what they do. For example, cardiologists deal with heart disease, gastroenterologists deal with digestive diseases, surgeons of all types deal with the surgical treatment of those diseases falling within their specialty, etc.

So it only remains to define the conceptually oriented physicians. In the mid 1960s, the term "primary physician" was defined as a physician who would be trained to manage the overall care of a patient in order to prevent the kinds of problems described above. This physician would be able to diagnose and treat many problems but would also know when to call on specialists. Since this physician would be responsible for the total care of the patient, the specialists would be subordinate in the decision making structure. Because of a broader knowledge of disease and because of knowledge of the patient's total condition, the primary physician was expected to have the authority to over-ride the specialist's recommendations if they seemed inappropriate to the situation.

But over the years, the term, "primary physician" has somehow become equated with a physician who only dealt with simple problems such as "colds," "flu," etc., and referred everything else. More and more, they are being viewed as "gatekeepers," physicians who simply let patients through the health care gate and then tell them which specialists to see.

Should patients be afraid of this? Yes. Medicine has the power and the knowledge to deal with almost any single problem a patient may have, *but the wisdom to use that power judiciously is lacking in the present structure.* Medical decision making skills have not kept pace with the technology.

Ironically, physicians who attempt to use medical resources judiciously for their patients are generally not paid as well. Their charges are the ones most frequently questioned by third party payers. In the attempt to control costs, more people are now getting involved in the control of individual patients.

This is another threat to quality of patient care from an entirely different angle. Now the privilege of making decisions about a patient's welfare is gradually being withdrawn from all physicians. Insurers (private and governmental) are forcing more and more of their decisions on the medical profession. Unfortunately, these decisions of the third party payers are mostly based on computer driven algorithms (recipes) which may work statistically for large groups but which often do not work for individual patients. This is what is so aggravating to many physicians today.

The wide variations among patients with the same disease is being forgotten.

Deciding on a diagnosis and then on appropriate treatment for each patient must be highly individualized most of the time, based on the patient's overall health status as well as on many psychological and social factors.

Keep in mind that there are only about ten symptoms, and these symptoms (with subtle variations) must be used to define three or four thousand diseases. What this means is that patients must be given the opportunity by their physicians to carefully and spontaneously describe their symptoms. Interruption of the patient's narrative must be kept to a minimum. Questions of the patient which either suggest the answer or limit the options for answering must be avoided. This information must then be interpreted in the context of the patient's total life situation, including age, sex, social and ethnic background, overall health status, etc.

Such interpretation requires highly developed communication and analytical skills. To use these skills properly requires that time spent with patients be allocated in accord with the complexity of the problem. This requires that physicians have the freedom to schedule their time spent with each patient as they perceive the patient's needs. The payoff comes from faster and more accurate diagnoses followed by more effective treatment.

Unfortunately, one of the thrusts of managed care programs is to increase physician productivity by either scheduling more patients per hour arbitrarily or by limiting fees per visit. This forces physicians to reduce time spent with each patient. According to a panel at the American College of Physician's Board of Governor's spring meeting, "Internists are being forced to see more patients, but spend less time with them." *The panelists felt that the growth of managed care contracts with discounts and capitated fees, fixed Medicare payments, and the rising cost of salary and benefits for office staff were responsible for this.*[3]

Basically, this is the inevitable outcome of viewing physician productivity in the same manner as industrial productivity, namely mass production and as many "widgets per hour" as is possible within the strictures of need and quality. However, patient care is different from industrial production. The "raw material" (human beings) coming into the system is not a constant as is the raw material used to manufacture a product. The production lines set up to manufacture a product are impossible to set up in a patient care setting (with a few exceptions such as mass

---

[3] American College of Physicians' *OBSERVER*, June, 1990, p. 39.

vaccination programs). The only place I have ever seen anything resembling production line medicine was in the military when large numbers of healthy young inductees were being examined for suitability for military service during World War II. This was a very demeaning experience. The only thing that saved that system was the youth and average good health of the inductees. In other words, they were not soliciting medical care. They were being examined only because it was required by the military.

Because the use of communication and analytical skills is not encouraged, what is developing in medicine is a kind of fantasy world, an Alice in Wonderland landscape, where right is left and up is down.

A few examples are in order.

A patient of mine in a nursing home became ill in the middle of the night. The attendants thought she was vomiting blood and called the paramedics to take her to the hospital emergency room. They then tried to call me. I was out of town at the time, and one of my partners took the call. He drove to the hospital at one o'clock in the early morning and saw the patient. There was no blood in her vomitus as tested by the laboratory. After examining her, he felt he could treat her in the nursing home and sent her back instead of admitting her to the hospital. She got along fine. In order to see her in the middle of the night, he spent fifty minutes driving plus about an hour in the emergency room.

Several weeks later, he got a letter from Medicare saying that they had denied the total bill because everything he did could have been done in the office.

They ignored the fact that the patient had already been sent to the emergency room when he was called. In addition, there was no way the patient could ever have come to the office even during the day. She had a severe generalized circulatory disease. Both of her legs had been amputated. Her heart, lungs, kidneys, and digestive tract were failing, and she required oxygen most of the time.

The strange thing about the story is that if he had hospitalized her that night, the government would have paid the hospital bill and his bill (both of which would have been much higher) without question.

This was explained to the Medicare carrier in detail by letter. Two months later he received payment in full (decided by Medicare) in the amount of $12.50. That was for two hours of his time in the middle of the night.

Another time, I was asked to examine a patient preoperatively to assess the risk of an operation. She had a disease that affects multiple organ systems including the lungs. The operation she was to have required a general anesthetic. The type of operation she was to have plus the fact that she would be put to sleep for it put her at risk of lung complications. Therefore, I obtained a chest x-ray as part of the preoperative examination.

Several months later, I received a notice from Medicare that they would not pay for the chest x-ray. They also stated that if I had already been paid by her, I was to refund the money. A copy of the letter was also sent to the patient. I responded by giving my reasons for obtaining the chest x-ray. Nine months later, after I had retired, I heard that the payment would be allowed. Dictating such letters, having them typed, mailing them, and waiting nine months or more for payment all add considerably to office overhead as well as to cumulative aggravation.

On another occasion, I submitted a bill to Medicare which included a charge for an injection of vitamin B_{12}. The patient had pernicious anemia, which requires B_{12} for survival. Usually, I teach patients to give their own injections of this drug, since it is much safer to administer than is insulin for diabetics.

But this patient would not administer it to himself. Somehow, the Medicare carrier overlooked the fact that the patient had pernicious anemia (they had received other bills prior to this one) and sent the patient a letter saying that I was giving him the medication unnecessarily. They did not contact me, but he showed me the letter.

There are other examples. A surgeon friend of mine admitted an elderly patient to the hospital the night before a major operative procedure so that the patient could have a number of tedious preoperative preparations done by the hospital staff.

The surgeon knew the rule that patients should do all these things at home the night before as a cost reduction measure. However, because of the patient's infirmities, the surgeon felt justified in bending the rules in what he thought were the patient's best interests. Not all patients are capable of doing these procedures effectively. In this instance, I agreed with the surgeon.

The outcome was that the surgeon had to pay the bill for the first day of the patient's hospitalization. He retired shortly after this incident although he had not planned to retire for several years. Our community lost a talented and experienced surgeon.

A last example involves a patient of mine who came to my office late one afternoon because of sudden onset of light headedness. Examination revealed that his stool was black and tested positive for blood. This indicated that he had lost a large amount of blood into his intestinal tract from a bleeding ulcer. I hospitalized him for blood replacement and treatment of the ulcer.

The next morning, I received a call from his insurance company asking when I was going to send him to surgery. I told them I didn't think he would need surgery, at least so far. Then they asked me how long I planned to keep him in the hospital, and I told them I didn't know, that it depended on whether the bleeding had stopped permanently. I told them anything I said at that stage would only be speculation.

Then they told me I had to give them a number, so I gave them an outlandish number of six weeks. They didn't like that, so I told them they could make a guess and put in any number that made them happier. They didn't like that, either.

Unlike some of my friends, I did not retire for several years after that, but I did stop calling insurance companies and getting twenty minutes of Muzak® before talking to somebody on the east coast about a patient in Minnesota. My patients were quite understanding of this and would make the calls themselves with the information I provided them. Then, if the insurers wanted to talk to me, they could call me. Fortunately, not too many did.

These sorts of things happen all the time to physicians everywhere, but the above examples are sufficient to give an idea of the adversarial relationship that is developing under the pressures of controlling costs. Physicians who are trying to make good decisions for their patients, to treat them as wisely and as inexpensively as possible, find other sources trying to take control from a distance.

This is becoming a critical problem in medicine today. Who is in control of the multiple decisions to be made? Is it primary physicians, specialty physicians, or third party payers? No one seems to know.

The result is the irrational interactions shown above, none of which is beneficial to the patient.

Chapter Nine

HOPING SOMETHING WORKS

The public would like to think, and mostly does think, that physicians approach medical decision making in an organized, rational manner. And most of the time they do, but there is room for much improvement. It is reassuring that the public still believes that there is a rationality behind the use of our technology. But this attitude might be changing.

For example, a woman in her mid-forties, a new patient to me, came for a routine physical examination. She proved to be in excellent health. Her reason for requesting the exam at that time was that her mother had died after a prolonged illness which included some time on artificial life support. After that experience, this young woman's response was to tell me she wanted an order placed on her chart that she should never be resuscitated or placed on artificial life support should anything happen to her. She wanted a blanket, unequivocal order to that effect.

I responded that I could not write such an order to cover all circumstances. I told her that I shared her views concerning futile treatment, but that intensive care resources were often worthwhile for a young, healthy person. I added that my behavior would be determined by the circumstances, and that I would use those resources only if I thought they would be beneficial to her. If not, I would not use them.

Basically, I told her that she would have to trust my judgement. I could not promise her that I would never use those resources in the course of any future treatment. She was so distraught by her mother's experience that she found my position unacceptable. She never returned to my office.

I teach a class for the general public on the implication of living wills. Hardly a class goes by without at least one or two of the students raising questions concerning prolonged and aggressive treatment of aging parents. They have considerable guilt concerning their decisions either to allow continued treatment or not allow it in a situation that is apparently hopeless. Many times they have cried in class as they relate the incidents.

Probably the best solution to the problem at the present time is for patients and families to be carefully informed of all the risks and benefits so that they are in a position to tell the physician of their wishes should things go badly. The living will legislation in many states partially addresses this problem.

In these kinds of critical situations, physicians, like most people, do not want to feel helpless. Unlike most people, however, physicians have a large variety of tools designed to put them in control. They do not have to feel helpless. Often, they can find something to do, even if it is only with the hope that it will work.

A problem seen frequently in medical practice today is called multiple organ system failure. It occurs in people who are critically ill, usually in people who already have chronic disability, and frequently in older patients. It often is a complication following extensive surgery although it may occur in other circumstances. It is a major problem because it is frequently irreversible (usually predictably so with a high degree of accuracy) and yet the patients can be kept alive for fairly long periods of time on artificial life support in intensive care units. As a general rule, the longer they require artificial life support, the less likely it is that they will survive. Needless to say, this causes great suffering to patients and their families. It is not an easy time for their physicians, either.

An example of this is demonstrated by a fairly common disease, aortic aneurysm. This consists of a swelling of the aorta, usually in the abdomen, and can be found either by physical examination or by a simple, noninvasive imaging technique called ultrasound. This disease is common enough that periodic examinations for its presence are recommended. It occurs most often in older people, many of whom, because of their age and associated diseases, have marginal heart function, kidney function, and lung function. When an abdominal aortic aneurysm is found and is of sufficient size, elective surgery is usually recommended.

Sometimes, however, the aneurysm begins to leak, which greatly increases the risk of surgery. When this happens, the patient will die within two months if the surgery is not done. That is a virtual certainty.

In the late fifties and sixties, we did not hesitate to recommend surgery to almost all patients with a leaking aneurysm despite the risk caused by various heart, lung, or kidney problems, because the alternative was certain death. In fact, I was involved in the care of many of these patients because of my subspecialty interest. The surgeon I worked with and I were well known in the hospitals large enough to deal with these kinds of problems. When we showed up together, the staff often suspected that a patient would die soon because the disease was serious and the techniques were primitive in the early years. One technique, for instance, involved wrapping the aneurysm with cellophane. This would irritate the tissues and presumably strengthen them. Sometimes it worked, but sometimes it caused so much pain that some patients committed suicide. This technique was soon abandoned in favor of placing grafts in the diseased segment. This was more successful but it remains a high risk operation when the aneurysm is rupturing.

In the early days, some of these patients survived, but many developed multiple organ system failure and died soon after surgery. We could say, then, regardless of the outcome that everything was done that could be done because the surgery was the limit of our capacity.

Today, surgery continues to be performed on these high risk patients because it is still true that without it they almost certainly will die within two months.

But there the similarity ends, because today, if high risk patients develop multiple organ system failure after surgery—and many do—there are many things that can be done for them, but sometimes to them, with the various forms of artificial life support that were not available in even the recent past. Oftentimes this is appropriate. Oftentimes it is not, and they die anyway after variable periods of suffering.

So the question today is, what should be done in these marginal situations? I want to emphasize that we are not talking about value judgements here but about hard medical decisions. These are not moral decisions. In medical practice, you must do what you think will work, not what you hope will work. If a physician thinks, after reviewing all the medical data, that placing a patient on some form of artificial life support will work, then it should be done.

But if the physician only hopes that it will help and places the patient on it, the physician is not only practicing poor medicine but is also being irresponsible and often cruel.

So what physicians of today have to recognize sooner than they often do is that critically ill patients ultimately reach a point where medicine can only prolong dying. It cannot help the patient any longer. At that point, it becomes purposeless to continue with curative treatment, since there no longer is any curative treatment for such patients. These are tough decisions to make, but they must be made.

My experience has been that most patients are terribly afraid of ending up on artificial life support when there is no longer hope of recovery. Many of them have talked to me about this when faced with high risk tests or treatments and have been quite explicit regarding their wishes. Others have talked to me about it when not faced with an imminent problem.

If we cannot resolve this problem of making difficult decisions based on the best data we can acquire, the alternative will be arbitrary rationing of services, probably based on a single variable such as age or general classification of disease types. To my mind, this would be indefensible. Making decisions based on one variable when many variables are involved not only is poor decision making but is grossly unfair. In medical practice, it would result in many patients who were treatable ending up untreated while offering no way to avoid giving treatment in other situations where the patient cannot be helped. Thus, it would not change the present deficiencies currently in our system which fall outside of the single variable (and this would be most of the deficiencies discussed in this book).

Pressures placed on physicians to do something when faced with the uncertainties of patient care are very powerful. One major source of pressure to do something is that physicians are haunted by the possibility of error. At best, a wrong decision will increase the likelihood that the patient's suffering will continue or even increase. At worst, the patient may die. Compounding this is the knowledge that it is impossible to be correct all the time. A physician who is correct 95 percent of the time is considered to be a very good physician, but that other 5 percent causes deep concerns and many sleepless nights.

An example of such pressures from my own experience involved a patient who had been a teacher of mine when I was a medical student and resident. In addition, he was my advisor on a research project I worked on for an advanced degree.

Twenty years after he was my teacher, he became my patient. At first, his health problems were relatively simple, but about five years after he became my patient, he developed a circulatory problem in his leg. It affected the circulation in his arteries and was of a type that could ultimately result in gangrene and amputation.

Naturally, he was concerned, but an examination revealed that gangrene was probably not imminent. The key word here, of course, is *probably*. Occasionally, the situation can change, and this is unpredictable.

If this were to happen, the circulation in his leg could become worse in a matter of minutes to hours.

Initially, his only problem was that when he walked a considerable distance, he experienced pain in his leg which went away when he stopped walking. Fortunately, he rarely needed to walk until his legs hurt. About the most distance he walked was while golfing, and he could walk 18 holes without difficulty or pain.

He wanted to know if he should have an operation to improve the circulation in his leg. This question raised several issues. The first was whether an operation would improve his ability to walk distances. It would, but he rarely walked far enough to precipitate the pain even without the operation. The second issue was whether an operation would prevent or delay the onset of gangrene. There are no data to indicate this, but there is always a possibility that it might make a difference in an occasional individual. Other issues were the risks of surgery to life, which was small, and the risk of surgery having no effect or even making the condition worse, which is unknowable.

This is the basic uncertainty of medical practice, and physicians, influenced by their role models in medical school, often choose to act in these situations. The pressures are there, and the decision can only be made once. I could not go back and do it again if the outcome were bad. Whatever the outcome of the treatment, I would have to live with the knowledge that I had advised it.

I advised against the surgery. If I had done otherwise, I would have been selecting the error of commission—choosing to do something the data did not support—to protect myself from the unlikely possibility that he might develop a gangrenous leg suddenly. This is sometimes called "treating yourself instead of the patient."

Time passed and his arterial disease progressed. His leg problems did not get worse, but he developed signs of the disease in his carotid arteries. These arteries supply the brain with blood. He did not have any symptoms, but examination revealed extensive obstruction. He then told me his greatest fear was that he would have a stroke before he died, and he made this very clear. He wanted to avoid this possibility and asked about the advisability of surgery. One surgeon advised him to have the surgery, and another surgeon said he would perform the surgery if the patient wanted it, but he would not make a recommendation one way or the other on the need for it. He told my patient that he would have to make the decision on his own. Both of these surgeons were highly respected academic surgeons with international reputations.

So he asked me for advice. By that time, he had been retired for a number of years and was at risk of a stroke, but his risk was more from the generalized arterial disease in his brain than from the carotid artery disease. He also had two other life threatening diseases by now—heart disease and a form of preleukemia. He knew all this, but he still made it clear that he was willing to take any risk to avoid a stroke. And because of his general condition, the risks of complications or death from surgery were very high.

Emotionally, this was a difficult decision for me to make. He was a friend, and I knew the risk of stroke was high whether he had the surgery or not. One of the complications of surgery could be a stroke. Nor did I know of any satisfactory evidence that successful surgery in his case would delay a stroke, although at that time this was a controversial issue.

So I advised against the operation on the basis of the data as I interpreted them and explained to him why I took that position. It was tempting, and would have been easier, to select an error of commission and do something, but that would have been bad decision making. Nor would it have helped him. Hoping for a good outcome does not make it happen.

Again, he took my advice, and he lived for several years after that. Ultimately, he died of a heart attack. He never had a stroke.

To me, his treatment was a success. There were a number of times during our relationship when I could have suggested some sort of treatment. Nobody would have questioned it even if he had died on the operating table. I mention this only to demonstrate how easily a bad decision can be made. Emotionally, it is easier to do something. I contend that selecting errors of commission is implicitly taught in medical schools when, by example, student physicians are taught to intervene almost uncritically with their technology.

The problem is that deliberately selecting error type actually increases total error. Usually, the error of commission is selected. Three things happen when physicians choose this path. First, unnecessary pain and suffering increase for the patient and family. Second, unnecessary death may occur. Few tests or treatments are risk free. Third, dollar costs rise. The illusion of being error free by selecting error type is a major factor in the rising cost of health care. It is also a major factor in reducing quality of care.

This is what frightens the public and causes such emotional upheaval when the question of critical care is raised.

Are there techniques or tools available that can guide physicians through these troubling moments, or are physicians more or less doomed to never get a good grip on the use of medical technology?

I believe that there are, and have been for at least twenty years, teachable skills available for physician guidance. Thus far, they are not being introduced into the curriculum adequately. There is little doubt that this large source of error could be reduced strikingly by emphasizing good decision making techniques in medical schools. Medical schools are where physicians learn medicine, and as long as the foundation for good decisions—the data from medical interviewing and a careful analysis of the patient's overall condition—is undervalued, bad decisions will continue to plague medicine.

There is one last area that minimizes error, and this may be the most misunderstood and undervalued of all. One of the greatest breakthroughs in medical testing has been in the esoteric study of a test's predictive value. As more is learned about this subject, it becomes increasingly clear that physicians can actually increase the reliability of the tests they use.

The predictive value of a test measures the likelihood that a positive result actually means that the patient being tested has the disease being tested for. Determining the predictive value requires knowing the usual things about the test being used, but also knowing the prevalence of the disease (how common it is) in the population being tested. This is critically important in clinical medicine because a physician can make a test either a useful or a worthless tool. The same test, depending on how a physician uses it can have a predictive value as high as 99 percent, which means that 99 out of 100 positive tests are true positives, or as low as 1 percent, which means that only one out of 100 positive tests is a true positive. In the second instance, the test results are in error in 99 out of 100 patients.

A knowledgeable physician can manipulate the predictive value of a test by manipulating the likelihood that the patient on whom he is going to use the test will fall into a population where the probability of the suspected disease being present is at least fifty percent. This is done with a careful history and physical exam. When the probability of a specific disease being present reaches 50 percent, the predictive value of subsequent tests reaches 95 percent.

An example of how this works is seen in how electrocardiographic stress testing is used. This is a test which consists of having an electrocardiogram done while exercising, usually on a treadmill at varying levels of physical stress. It is a test commonly performed to help clarify the cause of a very common symptom, chest pain, and can be a useful test when done for proper indications.

Unfortunately, it is often used to screen for the presence of heart disease in people who are at low risk of having heart disease. One such use of it is as a screen in people who are contemplating starting an exercise program. I have had many patients request such a test when they had no evidence of heart disease. Some insurance companies even require that it be done before issuing large life insurance policies. Some institutions market it as a tool to protect yourself from a heart attack if you are going to start an exercise program.

The problem is that it is not a reliable test under such conditions. If a patient starting an exercise program has, for example, a 5 percent chance of having a heart attack—the prevalence of heart disease in patients without symptoms in the population being studied—then this test has a predictive value of only 14 percent. This means that out of 100 positive tests, only 14 out of 100 tests will be true positive tests; 86 out of 100 will be wrong!

Contrast those figures with the following. The same test has a predictive value of 97 percent when used as a test for patients with typical chest pain associated with angina pectoris. Only three false positive tests out of 100 makes this a very good test in this instance.

Some people will say that it is important that the 14 people in the first example know that they have heart disease. That would be true except that no one knows which 14 out of the 100 with positive tests actually has the heart disease. To find out, further tests must be done on the entire 100 patients, and many are risky and invasive. Some people have argued that using this test as a screen actually may result in as many or more deaths from the testing than it saves lives by discovering the disease.

And it must be remembered that most of the complications from testing this low risk group would occur in people with no heart disease at all.

Again, I return to this point. Physicians who are trained in the disciplines involved in making medical decisions become very good at it. They recognize the value of technology, but they use it rationally.

At the present time, however, it seems that many physicians and some of the public place more faith in hoping for good results than in using sound, analytical methods to achieve them.

Chapter Ten

EVERYTHING HAS BEEN DONE THAT CAN BE DONE

We often used that expression back when there were so few diagnostic and therapeutic options available because it helped comfort patients and their families. It even comforted us as physicians. We were fairly safe in doing everything we could to treat our patients because what was available generally would not harm them, cause them much indignity, or cost very much.

At what point does a physician decide nothing else should be done? Years ago, it was easy to decide, because, quite literally, there was usually not much to do. One of the more poignant memories of my medical practice is of a patient I sat with as he died at home. This was in the 1950s. He was a policeman in his early 60s with high blood pressure and known, severe heart disease. I was called to his house late on a hot summer night because he was experiencing chest pain and shortness of breath. He had clearly had a serious heart attack, serious enough that the heart could no longer do its job. Even today, nothing could have been done for him. We called an ambulance, but he died before the ambulance arrived.

Everything had been done for him that could be done.

Contrast that with today. Choices now available to physicians are seemingly unlimited and extremely powerful with considerable potential to help, but also to harm the patient. One of the unfortunate legacies of the past is that there is still a great deal of pressure to do everything that *can* be done *to* patients rather than everything that *should* be done *for* them. We give them pills and injections. We test them. We probe them. We operate on them. We do everything possible, often even when it is uncalled for and unlikely to help.

We have come to this point because few really understand what it is that a physician actually does. Medical faculties do not even fully understand this. The emphasis placed on medical technology and subspecialization in teaching shows that medical educators view medicine as primarily a technological discipline. And while there is a highly sophisticated technological component to medical practice, patient care is primarily a conceptual discipline. Physicians make and sell decisions. *Everything else they may do is subordinate to this.* Unfortunately, the process of decision making has been devalued by medical educators, health insurance companies, and society as a whole. This is one of the main reasons the health care system is in such a mess today.

This is a frightening situation, and it only promises to get worse. I'm sure everyone knows someone who went to a physician with a complaint and later said that the physician did not listen or dismissed the complaint as being insignificant or treated it without sufficient explanation. This happens regularly because of a void in medical education, and it is later reinforced by the reimbursement patterns of insurance programs.

In this environment, it is not easy for a physician to come to a good decision, especially if the decision is to do nothing. I once was involved in a situation that seemed to dramatize this. A patient of mine who was in her nineties suffered from osteoporosis and periodically experienced severe pain. She did not have much interest in living any longer and would have welcomed death. When she first spoke with me, she said that, if I were to become her doctor, I would have to promise never to hospitalize her. I did not promise her that, but I did tell her that I would put her in the hospital only if I thought it would help her. She found this acceptable.

One afternoon this woman's daughter called me and said that her mother had apparently taken an overdose of sleeping pills the night before. It was obvious that she had planned this suicide attempt carefully because she "stole" the sleeping pills from a house guest some time before making the attempt. She had no prescriptions for them. When I arrived at her house, her condition was serious and I thought she would die.

Despite that, I decided not to hospitalize her. She had nursing care at home. Enough time had passed since she took the pills that I felt the hospital had nothing more to offer her than home care. There was also the possibility that, if she survived and awakened in a strange environment, she would experience a variety of adverse effects. This is common among elderly patients, so I thought it best for her to be home.

Since I thought she might die, I called the medical examiner's office.

They like to know when we think someone is going to die at home. Everything was routine until I was asked what was causing her death.

"Overdose," I replied.

That's when things got out of hand. They demanded that I hospitalize her. I refused on the basis that the hospital had nothing to offer that she did not have at home. As a matter of fact, her care requirements were such that I could not have justified hospitalization on the basis of Medicare regulations. So I hung up the phone and told the patient's daughter to expect the worst and suggested that she call her mother's lawyer for advice on keeping her at home.

Within minutes, paramedics and police were at the door, and police cars and emergency vehicles filled the yard.

For them, it was a very unusual situation, and, when we resisted sending her to the hospital, they began to suspect criminal intent. She was a wealthy woman so they wanted to be sure that she was not being killed for her money. They felt the best place to assure that would be in a hospital. The deputies wanted information about me, the patient, and her daughters.

Fortunately, one of the paramedics was quite reasonable and asked to see the patient. The nurse and I went with him, and he agreed that nothing could be done for her at the hospital more than was being done at home.

So they left. My patient survived without any permanent damage. I later found out that the sheriff's office had started a criminal investigation against me and the family.

That is but one example of how people often react to a decision to do nothing, even when it is the correct medical decision. A decision to do nothing in a drastic situation is usually interpreted as a moral decision rather than a medical decision. Yet, in most instances the evidence clearly indicates when a diagnostic or treatment option will not help the patient. That makes it a medical decision to do nothing, not a moral decision. Choosing to do something in those instances only increases medical errors which lead to more pain, suffering, sometimes death, and always higher dollar costs.

It is never easy to make such decisions. I recall thinking occasionally during my early days of practice that physicians should be like priests and forego having families. The time strictures of seeing patients, pondering their problems, responding to phone calls, studying, attending meetings, etc., were such that carrying out normal family responsibilities became very difficult. Only time and experience made it easier.

Bad decision making begins when physicians gather bad data, and this begins with the medical history. About 85 percent of the useful data for making decisions comes from the medical history. This is simply talking to patients to find out how they feel and what their complaint is. It sounds very simple, and there are even efforts to have computers take medical histories.

But, in reality, a medical history is a very dynamic and complex interaction that requires a skilled physician to elicit it. The data from it are very subjective and easily distorted or misinterpreted. Furthermore, communication and information gathering are influenced strikingly by variables such as the patient's social and educational background and psychological makeup as well as the skill of the physician taking the history. It comes as a surprise to most people that only about 30 percent of communication is verbal. Fully 70 percent is non-verbal and expressed through one's demeanor. One can gain an appreciation of this by listening to an interaction on an audiotape and then watching the same interaction on a videotape.

As an example of how subtle this interaction can be, I once participated in a study on interviewing techniques conducted by a graduate student as part of his Ph.D. thesis. I was being videotaped while taking a history, and there was a time limit on the interview. After about a half hour, I wondered how much time remained, so I sneaked a glance at my watch and continued the interview. Later, as we looked at the tape, it was obvious that the patient had seen me do this. He stopped talking in the middle of a sentence and then began again after a five second pause. Neither of us was aware of this time lapse during the interview, but while looking at it on the tape the patient said that he remembered interpreting my behavior as impatience and eagerness to finish. He resented this, and it affected the rest of his history.

On another occasion, a patient arrived before I did for a history that was going to be videotaped. The tape machine was on when he and his wife entered my office. He was in a wheelchair because of a stroke, and, since I had not arrived, he told his wife he had to go to the bathroom. She tried to dissuade him, but he replied with discomfort that if he did not go, he would wet his pants.

She was wheeling him out of the office when I arrived. She said they were going to the bathroom, and I told them to go ahead, there was no rush. But then he said he did not really have to go and would wait. Later, a behavioral scientist saw this tape and used it to demonstrate how dominant and powerful physicians were in their relationships with patients. Patients tend to try to please their physicians, even to the extent of ignoring discomfort.

Patients come to physicians with certain symptoms and also with certain concerns and fears. It is critical to the outcome that all of these things be learned by the physician, critical to making an accurate diagnosis and effecting successful treatment. All of these symptoms, concerns, and fears can only be learned from *listening to and observing* the patient during the interview. That is why 85 percent of the useful diagnostic information comes from the interview. 85 percent! Only 5 percent comes from testing such as imaging, blood tests, etc. Curiously, medical education emphasizes that 5 percent. The other 10 percent, of course, comes from the physical examination.

There are many examples illustrating this problem. It is well known among communication experts, for instance, that patients have certain priorities when they visit physicians. These priorities may relate to the severity of the symptoms, but often relate to fears and concerns. It is also well known that these priorities are usually directly related to the order in which the patient brings them up in the interview.

For this to happen, however, the patient must be allowed to relate the history in a relatively uninterrupted fashion. Despite this, numerous studies have shown that the patient is usually interrupted within twenty seconds by the physician who then takes over with controlling questions. The patient rarely gets back to the original narrative and the opportunity is lost.

Despite tremendous advances in knowledge concerning interpersonal communication, and despite all of the scientific and technologic advances in medicine, patient interviewing is still taught in basically the same way as when I was a medical student in the 1940s. So it is not surprising when patients complain that physicians do not listen to them or dismiss their complaints. Physicians still learn to take histories mostly from books, from lectures, and from seeing an occasional demonstration either live or on videotape in a lecture hall. They are rarely observed while taking a history.

When I was teaching, we tried to videotape medical students and residents as they took histories, but they disliked this experience intensely. I think they were embarrassed at seeing themselves learning a skill and not doing it well initially. Their resistance led to videotaping being largely discontinued as a teaching tool. Now they are only observed and critiqued a few times during their formative years. In the absence of videotape, they never see themselves function. This is a grave deficit in their experience. I believe that viewing one's self talking with a patient is the most powerful educational tool available for learning effective history taking.

A favorite expression of those opposed to formal instruction in communication skills was "Why do I need it? I've been communicating all my life."

When physicians make decisions on the basis of inaccurate data because they conducted an inaccurate or incomplete medical history, it sets the course of further testing and treatment of that patient for the foreseeable future.

The first and most important decisions in diagnosing and treating patients are made on the basis of the medical history. If information gathered from that source is wrong, a lot of other mistakes will be made before the physician is through with the patient.

Chapter Eleven

THE DECLINE OF PROFESSIONALISM

We are on our way to losing an integral group of physicians from the medical profession, namely the primary care physicians. Recall that the primary care physicians consist of general internists, general pediatricians, and family practitioners. Also recall that, by and large, programs in family practice are heavily dependent on general internists and general pediatricians for their educational content in these two very fundamental areas. As a matter of fact, physicians in all specialties, medical and surgical, are heavily dependent on general internal medicine and general pediatrics for their basic knowledge in patient care.

The commonly perceived crisis is cost, and indeed it is a major problem. Cost escalation must be controlled. If it is not, we will end up with either a bankrupt system or a two tiered system or both. None of the alternatives is desirable. The question is not whether to control costs but how to do it.

Unfortunately, the present injudicious and ineffective attempts to control costs are creating other problems that will soon loom as large or larger, such as a shortage of well educated, well motivated primary care (managerial) physicians.

So far, one of the outcomes of current arbitrary cost control methods is that physicians are being deprofessionalized. There is no question about this. This is very important to the future of patient care, because if physicians lose their professional status they will be unable to function effectively as physicians.

To understand what this means, one must examine the origins of the concept of "the learned professions." Historically, society has granted the status of "learned profession" to only three groups. These are medicine, law, and theology. Recently, it has been suggested a fourth group be added, namely military commanders in time of war. It grants the members of these groups the privilege of making major decisions "on the spot" on the basis of their accumulated knowledge in their area of expertise. They are held accountable for their decisions, but they still have considerable latitude.

Why is professional status granted to a group? Basically, it is granted if it seems to society that the body of knowledge encompassed by that group is either so complex or so arcane that only the members of that group have enough depth of knowledge to apply it wisely.

Professional status is not granted lightly. Certain privileges are granted in return for certain responsibilities being fulfilled.

First, the privileges. In the case of medicine, the privileges are as follows:

1. Special status is granted to members of the group. It is viewed as a prestigious group.

2. In general, "job security" is assured, as is reasonable income.

3. Because of the complexity or obscurity of the body of knowledge, the group (and members of the group) are granted considerable autonomy and authority in interpreting and applying it. In return for this, the group has the responsibility to control itself and to police itself.

4. Certain privileges are granted to the group to expedite performance of the occupation. For example, in medicine, the practitioner may touch the patient, ask personal questions, etc. Also, the practitioner must keep information so gathered in strict confidence. This is protected by law.

In return for the privileges, the public assigns certain responsibilities. Briefly, the public demands that the privileges be used responsibly and not for personal gain or for professional gain. The public demands that it be treated fairly.

It must be remembered that professional status of this type is granted by society, and what society grants, society can also take away. This is starting to happen now in medicine, but is it happening for the right reasons and will society gain by doing so?

The questions are, "Has the medical profession abused its privileges during recent decades?" and "Is the public correct in withdrawing professional status?"

The answers are difficult. It is my opinion that the medical profession has not dealt fairly with the public in many ways, and that it has not acted responsibly during the development of the current crisis.

I am not alone in this opinion. John F. Burnum, M.D., states it this way: "We have suffered a painful hurt to ourselves and our honor, and we have yet to recover. I think that medicine's highest priority in the 1990s should be to reestablish itself as a trustworthy and honorable profession."[1]

The second question is more difficult to answer. The public certainly has the right to withdraw professional status, since it is the grantor. But should they, and will it help to do so at this time? Who will fill the void that will be created? The reasons for professionalism are no less valid now than they have ever been. With all the complexities of modern medicine, I could argue that the need for true professionalism is greater now than ever.

An alternative to withdrawing professional status is for society to become more demanding that the medical profession fulfill its obligations more responsibly.

Many physicians are rapidly becoming demoralized because of the changes occurring today.

It has become clear to most physicians that they are not held in the same high public esteem as they once were. This knowledge is troubling to them. I see increasing disappointment and bitterness and some cynicism as a reaction to this.

Although there are many reasons for this loss of esteem, I believe that the common denominator is a change in the physician-patient relationship which has developed rather subtly with the increasing specialization of physicians and the increasing use of technology.

I also believe that physician demoralization is the result of their awareness (consciously or subconsciously) that their professional status is gradually being withdrawn. They can see this in many ways in their relationships with the public. Indirectly, this has the potential of adversely affecting their decision making.

One of the results of this is a loss of capable physicians, particularly those engaged in primary patient care. This is happening in a variety of ways.

More older physicians are retiring prematurely. They have tired of the constant hassle with what they regard as unreasonable demands on them. Some are leaving at the peak of their career when they have much left to offer their patients and the public at large. This is in sharp contrast to even the recent past when physicians continued to practice as long as they were able (and, unfortunately, sometimes beyond that point).

Increasingly, younger physicians are leaving careers in patient care to

---

[1] American College of Physicians' *OBSERVER*, June, 1990, p. 9.

pursue administrative roles. This is particularly true of those in primary care specialties. I have been surprised at the number who have returned to school to pursue business degrees. To me, this does not speak well for the future of medicine unless this tendency is reversed.

In addition, fewer medical school graduates are electing careers in primary care (general internal medicine, general pediatrics, and family practice).[2]

Let me quote a third year resident in internal medicine at the Mayo Clinic. "Dr. Cynthia Bubak sees herself as part of a "dying breed" of young physicians, one of the decreasing number who are interested in primary care medicine."[3]

These things are all inter-related. Many physicians are advising their family members and others who seek their advice not to choose medicine as a career in today's environment.

Such changes have serious implications for the medical profession and, more importantly, for the public.

---

[2]Greenberger, Norton J., American College of Physicians' *OBSERVER,* July–August, 1990, p. 2.

[3]Catherine LaMarca Stroebel, *The Mayo Alumnus,* Rochester, MN, Summer, 1990, p. 19.

Chapter Twelve

WHAT'S NEXT?

In the past, the state has had considerable influence on medical education through its licensing authority. In fact, this was one of the elements Flexner emphasized in his report which resulted in strengthening the state boards of medical examiners.

In recent decades, the situation has changed considerably. Now, the actual occupation of most physicians is no longer decided by the earning of the MD degree. Rather, the service a physician will deliver is decided later during several years of a hospital residency. *There is no structure incorporated into the specialty training programs to assure that the public interest is represented in the educational programs of the various specialties, either in content of the programs or in the numbers of students selected for the programs.*

All of the residency training programs are controlled by the national boards of the various specialties. They exert control through examinations for specialty certification. Thus, control of virtually all of graduate medical education (which today includes almost all medical school graduates) is fragmented among the various specialty and subspecialty certifying boards.

Most of the members of the boards are academicians and most of the boards are self-perpetuating. Despite the fact that they are called national boards, they are in every respect private organizations. *And yet, they control all graduate medical education in America!*

In my opinion, this is why change is hard to effect. I have spent increasing amounts of time over the last forty years trying to attract the attention of educators to the fundamental problems outlined in this book as well as to what seem to be obvious and definitive solutions. I have written and lectured on these subjects extensively. As the situation continued to worsen, my voice became ever more strident.

The recurring criticism of my positions is that they are not new, that they have been proposed before. Of course they are not new. They have been proposed by others since at least 1910. *That is the disaster. They are proposed by a variety of people but ignored by those in control of the education of physicians.* It has been like punching a pillow all these years. I have mainly quoted from Flexner and Millis in this book, but there are many other reports of a similar nature, all ignored.

And I am not alone in these positions at the present time. Many physicians and other health professionals support these views. I suppose the proponents and opponents are close to equal in numbers. *Unfortunately, the proponents do not hold the academic power throttle and have difficulty being heard.*

The biggest obstacle to effecting change, however, is apathy of the bulk of the medical profession as well as the public at large. This apathy must be overcome if we are to achieve any results. I hope this book is successful in doing this.

The difficulty encountered by those seeking educational reform is demonstrated in another way in the quotation to follow.

"Any contemplated move by a medical school toward true structural reform must also consider a shift in the existing balance of power within the school toward those who are most interested in, and responsible for, medical student education. . . . *By failing to address fundamental organizational issues, medical educators risk perpetuating the 'history of reform without change.'*" (emphasis added)

The above quotation was from a paper published in the Journal of the American Medical Association on February 27, 1991.[1]

"Reform without change" summarizes the history of medical education in the United States for at least the past forty years.

This book was written to attract attention to what has happened in American medicine this century and to what is happening now. It relates the history of medical practice during my professional lifetime as I and many others perceived it. I was involved in much of the action in my area (Minnesota) which was a pioneer state in many ways.

This is an appeal to the general public, although I hope the medical profession will also get involved. If it gets enough attention from both groups, perhaps it will force scrutiny of the problems described in it. Look at it as a review of the mistakes we made collectively (physicians and the public). We dug the hole we are in, and the best way to get out

---

[1] Cantor, Joel C., et al, Medical Educators' Views on Medical Education Reform, *Journal American Medical Assn.*, Feb. 27, 1991, p. 1002.

will be to work cooperatively on solutions. This is the most likely approach to succeed.

I am asking for action from anyone or any group concerned about the future of American medicine. I am not one who says it was the best the world has ever seen, but it was pretty good. Certain parts of it were the best. Some parts were not.

The task will be difficult, but none of the easy solutions have worked nor are they likely to work in the future.

What is needed is someone of the stature of Lincoln or Churchill to organize and to achieve the solutions.

The importance is such that, if we fail the task, I am not sure I would want to be a recipient of medical care in another ten to fifteen years. On the other hand, if we succeed, medical care will be superior to anything ever seen before, not only technologically, but socially as well.

One last word of encouragement. I asked a friend of mine who was an executive in a company whose business was totally unrelated to health care to read a draft of this book and give me his opinion about it. He said he found it to be interesting and informative, but that it made him feel that the problems were almost insoluble.

I do not want to leave that impression. I believe they are readily soluble if the recommendations of the following chapters are implemented. Getting them implemented will require difficult negotiations, to be sure, but a demanding public can do it. And the public must realize that it will take time because it is an educational solution. The Flexner revolution related to educational reform also, and it took time to achieve. But what a payoff resulted from it. The reforms I suggest will be faster of achievement and will have an even bigger payoff, a "double whammy," so to speak. They will assure better utilization of the benefits of the Flexner revolution and will also provide more rational patient care across the board through the medium of better overall management of care by well educated primary physicians.

Chapter Thirteen

FACING UP TO REALITY

As it turned out, the Flexner revolution was solely a technologic revolution. This was not his intent. He made a second recommendation which was either overlooked or ignored. Even in 1910, as bad as things were, he saw the danger in overemphasizing technological development without also improving physician education in other areas. This is what he said.

"So far we have spoken explicitly of the fundamental sciences only. They furnish, indeed, the essential instrumental basis of medical education. *But the instrumental minimum can hardly serve as the permanent professional minimum* (emphasis added). It is even instrumentally inadequate. The practitioner deals with facts of two categories. Chemistry, physics, biology, enable him to apprehend one set; *he needs a different apperceptive and appreciative apparatus to deal with the other, more subtle elements. Specific preparation in this direction is much more difficult;* (emphasis added) one must rely for the requisite insight and sympathy on a varied and enlarging cultural experience. Such enlargement of the physician's horizon is otherwise important, for scientific progress has greatly modified his ethical responsibility. His relationship was formerly to his patient—at most to his patient's family; and it was almost altogether remedial. The patient has something the matter with him; the doctor was called in to cure it. Payment of a fee ended the transaction. *But the physician's function is fast becoming social and preventive, rather than individual and curative.* (emphasis added) Upon him society relies to ascertain—and through measures essentially educational to enforce—the conditions that prevent disease and make positively for physical and moral well being. *It goes without saying that this type of doctor is first of all an educated man.*[1] (emphasis added)

If this advice had been followed at the time, and subsequently, many of the problems we face today could have been averted.

---
[1] Abraham Flexner, *Medical Education in the United States and Canada,* 1910, p. 26.

What Flexner was saying in the modern context is that medicine is as much or more a social science than a technological science and that the practicing physician needed to be knowledgeable in both fields to be effective. This was a tremendous insight back in 1910.

It has always been a curiosity to me that only his first recommendation was followed. I suspect the reason was that physicians and public alike were swept up in the euphoria of the new discoveries to the extent that disease became the only enemy. Once this happened, it followed logically that if (and a BIG if) disease could be eradicated by technologic improvements, all of the maladies of mankind could be controlled. Perhaps the enthusiasm peaked with the declaration of "war on cancer" and the "heart disease, cancer, and stroke" programs of the late sixties and early seventies.

No one denies the value of the advances of recent years. Everyone stands to benefit from them at one time or another on an individual basis. Looking at it in the aggregate, however, there are two fallacies in our modern approach to medical education and patient care.

The first is that day-to-day medical practice is approached as if most of the problems are potentially life threatening when, in reality, they are not. This is sometimes called the "looking for zebras in a cow pasture approach." It is true that day-to-day medical practice does include many severely disabling conditions, either acute or chronic. The modern practitioner must be taught to deal with these conditions effectively through better understanding of how to diagnose and treat them properly without the diagnostic and therapeutic excesses so commonly seen today. For this to happen, skills in understanding human behavior and skills in decision logic must be better taught in medical schools to the physicians who are responsible for most of the decisions.

The second fallacy is that we think that application of modern therapeutic technology has been responsible for the dramatic increase in life expectancy this century. In reality, most of the increase has been due to public health measures to control infectious diseases (primarily childhood diseases, childbirth fever, and cleaning up the water and food supply). Actually, up to the late seventies and early eighties, anyone attaining thirty years of age could expect little greater life expectancy than someone attaining thirty years of age in the 1920s. During the 1980s, life expectancy has increased a few years for those past thirty. However, no one quite understands why, and most think it is related to life style changes in the public at large rather than to treatment of specific diseases. The possible exception to this is the treatment of hypertension, which has been remarkably effective.

These errors in thinking represent the problem and are the keys to the solution of the problem. *The high cost of medical care is due to the tendency of physicians to think as they have been taught to think.* That is, to look relentlessly for life threatening illness by utilizing, inappropriately, vast amounts of diagnostic and therapeutic technology to try to find and eradicate diseases with low probability of being present. This not only increases direct costs (the cost of the tests and treatment) but also indirect cost (prolongation of disability by treating the wrong problem as well as prolongation of disability through anxiety caused by the uncertainties created by excessive testing). Another indirect cost is the cost of treating new illnesses caused by inappropriate testing and treatment.

The errors I am discussing are not related to laziness or greed on the part of physicians. Rather, they are related to the emphasis of medical educators on the teaching of "high-tech," "acute care" medicine almost exclusively. I agree it must be taught, but not to the exclusion of the other half of necessary medical knowledge.

Teaching the entire breadth of clinical medicine is impeded by the fact that the great majority of teachers in medical schools are narrow specialists. There is a serious lack of teachers with a broad outlook. They are absent because there is no reward system for them. They are not readily promoted. They do not sit on key departmental committees. They are not accorded respect by their faculty colleagues.

This is not overlooked by the medical students. Consequently, in the absence of such role models in the medical education scene, there has been a flight to the subspecialty areas where there are plentiful role models.

It has often been said during the past decades that our technology has surpassed our ability to deal with it. I agree that this is the problem, although it needn't be. Compare medical technology to nuclear energy. We have the same problems dealing with both of them. We have made bad choices in each field. Since I am not a nuclear expert, I will not presume to define how that field should be handled.

But I do know the field of clinical medicine. I believe strongly that our technologic advances have been brilliant, and I believe we are better off for them, but only if they are used properly. This is the real issue.

Why did these problems develop in medicine? In my opinion, it relates to the fact that we are in the midst of a scientific revolution as defined by Thomas Kuhn,[2] a revolution in which a new outlook replaces the old one.

Basically, the existing paradigm (structure, belief) in medical education is being attacked in this book as well as by others. Important changes are being recommended. Effecting such change is always difficult, because the changers are challenging the status quo, and the supporters of the status quo currently hold the power throttle. In the case of clinical medicine, it is the academic community, heavily invested in the current system, who have been "stonewalling" most recommendations for substantive change in the educational system since at least the early 1960s.

The medical profession and society have now had eighty years to decide to follow the second recommendation of the Flexner report.

Perhaps it is time to examine what this would entail and then do it.

The seriousness of our present situation in patient care has been emphasized and reemphasized throughout this book. The time has come for action. What can we do?

What we can do now is what should have been done years ago. It will not be easy, and it will take time to accomplish. The time factor is the main reason that the many other attempted solutions (all of which are failing) have been tried during the past two decades. They appeared to be easier and faster to implement. And they were. The only trouble is that they don't solve the problems. Not only do they fail to reduce cost, but, over time, they will reduce quality. I offered some solutions twenty-four years ago. I was told that the solutions I was proposing were substantive, but that they were too slow in that they would take fifteen or twenty years to accomplish. *Well, twenty-four years have gone by and the problems still beg for solution.*

Worst of all, so far none of the solutions implemented to date have even reduced dollar cost. In fact, dollar costs have continued to rise much faster than the overall cost of living.

Things are desperate.

Correcting current problems will be difficult and will take time if it is to be done properly. *There is no "quick fix."* One reason things got so bad is that we panicked and pursued overly simplistic solutions to a complex problem. We only made it worse. And, if we continue on our present course, we will continue to make it worse. Effective solutions will

---

[2]Thomas S. Kuhn, *The Structure of a Scientific Revolution, 2nd Edition,* University of Chicago Press, 1972.

require deliberate, thoughtful action by an informed public and medical profession.

It must never be forgotten that human beings are highly complex organisms and that their illnesses are usually unique to each individual. The disease itself is not the only determinant of outcome. Rather, it is the disease occurring in an individual with a unique physical and emotional capacity which must be dealt with. This is the reason why decisions may be different for treatment of the same disease in different people. This is the reason that decision making must be tailored to the individual patient with due consideration of all the variables in that patient's physical makeup and environment. This is the reason that simple treatment algorithms (standard recipes for diagnosis and treatment) will not work at our present stage of knowledge and probably will never work. This is the reason that modern primary physicians (the managers of the overall care of the patient) must be educated in other areas than basic biomedical science as well as continuing with their present educational programs.

In the words of John Millis, "If we further destroy continuity and comprehensiveness by thinking of the job of the primary physician as defined by primary care (Millis defines primary care as limited to first level acute care and defines the primary physician as the patient's manager through all levels of care), I shudder for the future of the medical care of American citizens. It won't be very good; in fact, it will probably be a lot worse than it was pre-1966."[3]

To start, let's look at some of the current ideas as to why we are in trouble.

Perhaps the most common one is that the availability of our technology is a prime factor causing the high cost. This is true, but, I believe, only if it is used inappropriately. *If medicine is like anything else, and if our technology is effective, (and it is) it should reduce cost if used properly.* This is a basic truism.

A second idea is that malpractice problems of physicians are major factors in the cost escalation through the mechanism of generating unnecessary tests, treatments, and hospitalizations to protect against lawsuits. This may be a small factor in raising aggregate cost, but it is not a major one. It is also a correctable one.

---
[3]John Millis, Address to the Society of Teachers of Family Medicine, *Family Medicine Times,* January, 1976, 8:7–12.

The expansion of our aging population is often cited as a cause of the cost escalation, and this is true. The aged have more illness and use a disproportionately large portion of our total resources. Although this will continue to be true, I believe a significant proportion of the resources prescribed for the aged are probably inappropriate as judged by effectiveness and need (appropriateness of utilization). In other words, does much of what is done for aged patients actually benefit them? There are abundant data that imply the aged are recipients of many unnecessary tests and treatments. If this could be corrected, cost would be reduced and quality improved. And this overutilization can be corrected by improving the education of primary physicians.

Payment mechanisms have been blamed for the rising cost. Accusations have been made that the incentives are for overutilization in the fee for service system, that the more the physician does, the higher his income becomes. This is true.

It is beginning to be said that the incentives in prepayment (HMOs) are wrong in that they encourage underutilization. The less the physician does, the higher his income becomes. This is also true.

National health insurance is advocated by some on the premise that placing physicians on salary and removing all incentives would obviate both of the above concerns. This is also true.

Most importantly, however, is that in all three of the above settings, the final performance of the physician is dependent solely on skill and integrity, not on payment mechanisms. In the absence of skill and integrity, unscrupulous or incompetent physicians are easily able to "game" any of the payment mechanism systems.

The ultimate success of any payment mechanism is totally dependent on the physician's ability and willingness to make objective decisions in the patient's interest unrelated to the physician's personal gain. This is really what professionalism is all about and why the "learned" professions have been sanctioned by society over the centuries.

An interesting example which illustrates this point occurred when a former patient of mine returned to me for a second opinion. He had developed heart disease and suffered from angina pectoris (chest pain when he exerted himself). He had been receiving his medical care from a closed panel prepaid group practice, and his physician had recommended coronary artery bypass surgery. His question of me was whether I agreed with this opinion. It was a fascinating situation to me. His physician was in a group where it is alleged that they are paid more for doing less and I was in a fee-for-service environment where it is alleged that I would be paid more for doing more. After studying him, I recommended delaying surgery until non-surgical treatment was explored to a greater extent. There was no question that he had coronary artery disease and angina pectoris. It was also possible that he would require surgical treatment at some time in the future. My recommendation was that he continue with medical treatment for a longer period of time. I explained this to him, and he returned to his physician.

I learned later that he decided to go ahead with the surgery.

The point of this is not who was right or wrong in this situation. I'm not sure if we will ever know that, since we couldn't do it both ways. The important point is that the payment mechanism did not affect either his physician's decision or mine. We both made our decisions independently of how we were paid, and we each made decisions based on how we interpreted the data, not on the payment incentives.

This is why I believe that payment mechanisms are irrelevant to the solution of our problems and are irrelevant to cost reduction. *There may be reasons why one payment mechanism or another may be more satisfactory in one setting or another. However, that is a different and unrelated argument.* When it comes to cost control, (and remember, the total definition of cost is pain and suffering from prolonged disability, unnecessary death, and dollar cost), selection of one payment mechanism over the other is not the answer.

So, what is the answer?

It is to recognize that the powerful and sophisticated tools available today call for equally powerful and sophisticated decision making by physicians so that medical technology will be used for maximum benefit with least harm to patients.

Instead, the solutions of today are such devices as requiring that the insurer be called for permission to do a test, admit a patient to the hospital, or perform a surgical procedure. This is then resolved by the recipient of the phone call looking at a prediagrammed recipe (algorithm) and usually making a decision. Sometimes consultation is had on the telephone with a physician who does not know the patient. Then, if agreement is not reached, some form of arbitration is used.

It embarrasses me as a physician and as a human being that the above solutions are even taken seriously, given the high stakes for the patient on whom the decisions are being made. Much more likely to succeed is to better prepare physicians who are directly responsible for the care of the patient to handle the new environment in which they find themselves.

The implementation of Flexner's second recommendation and those of the Millis Report will require the cooperation of the public at large working through their elected representatives, the community of medical practitioners, and the medical education establishment. It will require all of these participants because not only will the medical school and graduate school curriculum have to be augmented but postgraduate courses will have to be established for physicians in practice who did not have the benefit of such education while in school.

This is what must be done:

1. Continue present educational programs for primary physicians in biomedical science. They must be broadly knowledgeable regarding diagnosis of illnesses and of availability and effectiveness of treatment options.

2. The following must be added to the educational programs.

   A. They must be taught how to recognize the statistical traps often seen in medical writing. Breast cancer in women under fifty is an example. There is ongoing argument as to lifetime risk of getting the disease as well as what is the optimal frequency of mammography. The question is how can physicians provide informed consent when recommending mammography as a screening exam.

   B. The study of modern decision logic must be emphasized. The meaning of predictive value to the clinician as a tool for determining how and when to select certain forms of testing must be mastered by all primary physicians. The limitations of using tests for screening purposes must be made clear. Error management must be emphasized.

   C. The teaching of communication theory and interpersonal communication must be updated.

   D. Behavioral science applicable to clinical medicine must be made part of the curriculum. This should include those portions applicable to various age groups, especially adolescents and the elderly.

   E. Their responsibilities in assuming a managerial role must be demonstrated and emphasized in the programs.

   F. Their teachers must be exemplary role models in the practice of primary care medicine.

The accomplishment of the above will require impressive changes in the structure of the educational establishment and of the practitioners in the community. It will necessitate recruiting exemplary clinicians and teachers to medical school faculties for the purpose of teaching. In order to recruit such faculty, the departments will have to first demonstrate to them that they will have the respect of their colleagues on the basis of what they do. *The tangible demonstration of this will be faculty rank comparable to the researchers and subspecialists. Appointment to key departmental committees will also be a requirement. Assurance of promotion when earned must be given. Suitable office and patient care space must be provided.*

In addition to the above, there will have to be similar changes in the structure of medical practice in the community. This will be required in order to recruit quality students into the programs. They must be recognized for what they do. They can no longer be looked upon merely as "gatekeepers" for the system. They must be recognized as the critical managers of care for their patients with the knowledge and authority to accept or reject the recommendations of technologically oriented physicians.

The changes in the structure of academic and community medicine will be difficult to achieve, but it must be done if we are to successfully effect the changes necessary to reverse the adverse changes in medical practice of the past several decades.

How can it be done? That is what the next chapter is about.

Chapter Fourteen

A CALL TO ACTION

The Report of the Citizen's Commission on Graduate Medical Education in 1966 remains the most substantive document recommending reforms in current medical education to date. The term "Primary Physician" was coined by this group. They state, "The medical literature is full of articles lamenting the failure to develop a substantial corps of well trained primary physicians. Why, then are there so few of them?" They list three major reasons which include many of the reasons discussed in this book. Their conclusion was "All three of these difficulties can be overcome, but heroic work will be required. *It is time for a revolution, not a few patchwork adaptations.*"[1] (emphasis added).

Now, even more than in 1966, revolutionary changes are required.

How can the changes recommended in the previous chapter be effected?

It will require action by the public at large, probably through their elected representatives. This could be at either state or national level.

The first step would be to set up a study committee under the auspices of the government. Although this could be at either the state or federal level, doing it at the state level would probably be best initially. It most certainly will require that all affected parties be involved in the negotiations. This includes representatives from the public at large, the business community, insurers, government, the academic medical community, and physicians practicing in the community. Of the community physician group, there should be representatives of the technologically oriented physicians as well as representatives of each of the primary care specialties.

The negotiations will be difficult, because each group is heavily invested in the outcome. Some of the groups are also heavily invested in the status quo. These problems will have to be overcome, which may take time and understanding.

---

[1] *The Graduate Education of Physicians,* Council on Medical Education, American Medical Assn., Chicago, IL, p. 37–38.

There is no easy way to do it, but it must be done, and it must succeed. Failure would be devastating to all of the involved parties.

Let's speculate on the outcome if this is not done, or if it is tried and fails.

The outcome of failure would be a continuation of our present course. What can we then expect?

Continuing cost escalation would be a certainty. This would inevitably be followed by arbitrary rationing of care. Access to care would be further limited. The number of uninsured and inadequately insured would increase. Quality of care would become unacceptable. Initially, the public would feel the major portion of the burden. I suspect that we would develop even more of a two-tier system of care than we now have.

Physician discontent would continue to increase far beyond that of today. We are already seeing a mini-flight from medical practice. Many physicians are advising students who ask their advice not to enter the field of medicine today. This includes advice to their own children.

Unless we resolve the problems I have outlined, the "mini-flight" from medical practice, and especially from primary care, will become a stampede.

How can successful negotiations be assured?

For success to happen will require great understanding on the part of all members of the committee. Each member will have to realize that every other member has some legitimate positions. Also, each member will have to be willing to accept some compromises during the negotiations.

I said early in the book that there was enough blame for everyone, physicians, hospital administrators, third party payers, and the public. I truly believe that to be true. The committee members of each group must keep that in mind during the negotiations. Any perceived transgressions of the past must be forgotten. Everyone must be concerned only with improving the future.

I have been particularly critical of the educational establishment throughout the book, and I believe that criticism to be justified insofar as to how they have carried out their educational responsibilities. However, in fairness, I must point out that they have carried out their research responsibilities exceedingly well. Most of our advances can be credited to their work. I say this because I do not feel that this group should be displaced. We need their efforts in the field they do best, which is research and the teaching of the technologically oriented physicians. My only position relative to them is that they must relinquish teaching authority over educational programs for primary care physicians to other educators who understand the educational needs in these areas better than they do.

The main reason nothing has been done over the past twenty to thirty years is because of the sensitivity of the subject. To establish a formal program pointed toward an entirely new method of educating primary physicians for the responsibility of being overall managers of patient care and then giving them responsibility for such management is indeed revolutionary. Basically, it will change the hierarchical structure of academic medicine and of medical practice.

For this reason, each of the health care provider groups represented on the committee will have reason to feel threatened by the changes the committee is seeking to effect. These fears will have to be addressed at the outset and overcome.

I believe it can be done. To accomplish it, the chair of the committee will have to be chosen with care. The position will require broad knowledge of the problem, fair mindedness, and courage. Its occupant should have the respect of all the committee members.

The goals will have to be defined at the outset. To my mind, there should be only two goals and the committee should not diverge from them. The first should be to define a new body of knowledge to augment the education of primary physicians. The second should be to set up a system for implementing the incorporation of the new body of knowledge into the educational programs. This must include plans for the education of the teachers of the new programs.

Any other specious question which may come up (i.e., remuneration, status, etc.) should be ruled out of order in order to prevent the committee from getting hopelessly mired in abstractions. There will be plenty of time to consider these "side issues" at a later date. While they are important, they should have second priority.

I would recommend that the study committee be formed by state legislatures and that the chair be appointed by the legislature. The other committee members should be appointed after consultation between the chair and the organization representing each group.

The committee should have a specific charge and should be required to report at stipulated intervals. It should be authorized to seek consultation as necessary.

It should be protected from political pressures.

Chapter Fifteen

CONCLUSION

There is no doubt that the health care system in the United States needs to be carefully examined and changed.

The three plans with which I am most familiar are the plan in Minnesota, the Clinton plan, and the plan put forth by the American Association of Retired Persons.

All of them have commendable features, but it is my opinion that the plan devised by the American Association of Retired Persons is the most carefully thought out and is the most realistic in terms of implementation and financing.

However, all three of them have a common weakness. The weakness is that, while they all are strong advocates of using primary physicians in a leading role, none of them really understand what the role of primary physicians should be in modern medical practice.

They only view primary physicians as "gatekeepers" to be used to control utilization by controlling access more or less arbitrarily.

They fail to understand the key role primary physicians must play as managers of the total care of their patients at all levels of patient care (primary, secondary, and tertiary).

They fall into the trap deplored by John Millis who emphasized over and over again that primary physicians were more than "primary care" physicians. The Millis Report was very explicit that an entirely new type of primary physician be educated to assume the heavy responsibilities of patient care management in the context of modern medical practice. It advocated an entirely new educational program for this specialty.

Actually, Millis regretted coining the term "primary physician" because it was so universally misunderstood. I agree, and would agree with a friend of mine who feels that the term "principle physician" be substituted.

Thus, the common weakness of all of the plans is that they advocate training larger numbers of primary physicians, but in the same mold as in the past. This will not be effective for the reasons outlined in this book. Until this deficit is acknowledged and corrected, all of the plans will fail in their goal of achieving increased quality at lower cost. In fact, the reverse will happen, namely, decreased quality at increased cost, because as quality goes down, cost inevitably goes up. This is as true in patient care as it is in industry.

That is why I wrote this book. I wanted to give the public a look at the "nitty gritty" of patient care.

I hope that this will stimulate action to redefine and reeducate the primary physician. If this happens, health care reform will work, and all of the American public will receive better care than ever before.